The Weiwu at Dafuzhen

Qinghua Guo and Yuyu Chang

The Weiwu at Dafuzhen

Unseen Details of Chinese Vernacular

Edition Axel Menges

The publication of this book has been made possible by a grant from the Faculty of Architecture, Building and Planning of the University of Melbourne.

ISBN 978-3-936681-94-9

Printing and binding: Graspo CZ, a.s., Zlín, Czech Republic

Design: Axel Menges
Layout: Helga Danz

Even though I have been interested in vernacular architecture for a long time, I only started to work on this book in July 2014. This research was triggered by two events: first, a weiwu at Dafuzhen (1870) caught my attention in early January 2012 during a field trip in Fujian with Yuyu Chang who was a visiting scholar at our university; and second, the university requested that the relationship between the host and the guest should be a research partnership

This book is the result of our joint-teaching and research project. The rich and diverse vernacular architecture of China has provoked admiration, but it is seldom analysed as a key to our understanding of Chinese architecture. There were three principles when I designed the project: it must be a detailed case study; a documentation in graphic form with notes adhere to; and the architecture must be understood in planning contexts.

The study of this particular case has raised numerous questions among which is that its design is unknown. A step-by-step investigation of Dafuzhen's various features has provided a great deal of information. This book presents the weiwu in a tectonic and technical sphere. Our study on building and setting has led to an understanding of the reasons for architectural forms and planning.

This book consists of three parts. Part I puts Dafuzhen in a context. Part II deals with Dafuzhen from two perspectives: planning and architecture. Part III concerns details at design level. As demonstrated in this study, first, water management played an important role in overall design and planning; second, the weiwu was closely related to a group of Chinese architecture typologically.

I am grateful to He Jingping of the Fujian Provincial Administration of Cultural Heritage, Liang Wenbin and Huang Chunlin of the Youxi Museum for their support and the Dafuzhen residents for their cooperation. I would like to thank the third-year architectural students from Zhejiang University, who recorded the Dafuzhen in measured drawings. Gunnar Almevik of the University of Gothenburg, Sweden, and Ross Berryman of the University of Melbourne, who participated in our joint-teaching program in Fujian, I thank them for allowing me to use some of their photographs. I thank also Xuxuan Sun for assisting me to edit the measured drawings for publication.

Qinghua Guo, February 2016

Qinghua Guo is professor of Asian Architecture and Planning at the University of Melbourne. She initiated the project and carried out this research book. Yuyu Chang is associate professor in the Architecture Faculty of Zhejiang University of Science and Technology in Hangzhou, who coordinated with the locals and supervised the recording of the Dafuzhen in measured drawings.

Introduction

Weiwu in a context

The discovery of Tanshishan site near Fuzhou, the provincial capital of Fujian, reveals a settlement where semi-underground circular buildings belonging to the late Neolithic and Bronze Age were found. While the excavated architectural remains from the Qin dynasty (221–206 BC) down to the Ming dynasty (1368–1644) in the region are limited and the architectural history of the region remains un-reconstructed, there are many buildings survived from the Ming-Qing period (Qing 1644–1911).

In Fujian, there are mountains and valleys covered with dense forests and watercourses. The topography of Fujian is divided by the mountain chains and the river valleys into five regions: north, south, east, west and middle. This may have been a crucial factor in stimulating cultural regionalism. Linguistically, Fujian's inhabitants speak five dialects as they entered Fujian from different localities, in the process of migration from the distant past to the Qing dynasty. Architecturally, Fujian's built environment is diverse, as the communities were independent, and isolated enough for security. The formidable mountains, various dialects and traditional customs helped to maintain the strong architectural cultures inherited from their respective ancestors.

Fujian has a warm and humid subtropical monsoon climate – hot in summer with abundant rainfall and cool in winter. Temperatures average 20°C in summer and 12°C in winter. This helps explain why ventilation and drainage are the key in architectural design and settlement planning.

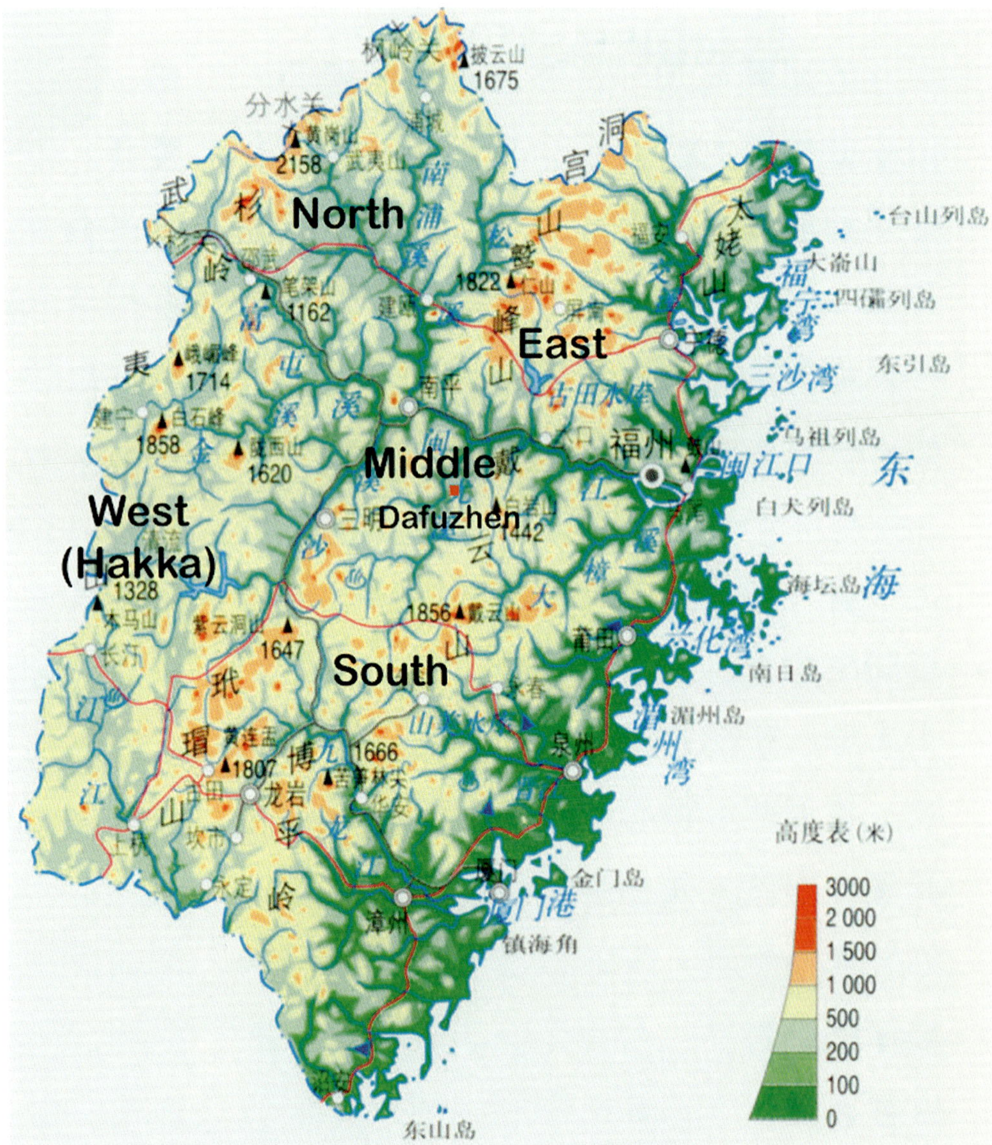

1. Dafuzhen in Fujian, China.
2. Fujian province, 121,400 sq. km.

3. The migration of peoples from the north across the mainland throughout history.
4. Weiwu at Dafuzhen.
5. Tulou at Chuxi.

Two main types of residential architecture have dominated the architecture in the Fujian region. Known as tulou and weiwu, they were developed in parallel. Both are designed for communal living, but are distinct from each other in terms of setting, layout, form and size. A good deal is known about tulou, the Hakka's architecture, which has been inscribed as UNESCO World Heritage in 2008, but existing scholarship on weiwu is lacking.

The term »weiwu«, meaning »enclosed house«, is used by modern scholars to describe a type of enclosed compounds consisting of timber-framed, single-storey buildings. The weiwu at Dafuzhen is a characteristic example. In this study, we are primarily concerned with Dafuzhen weiwu, supplemented by other weiwu in the region, which are similar or relevant. Where possible the design method and craftsmanship used in weiwu are sourced locally in Fujian.

The other weiwu referred to in this study are Xiao's old estate, Shujing, Guangyu, Sibao and Zhengshi.

Weiwu at Dafuzhen

Located at Pingzhai belonging to the Youxi county in central Fujian, Dafuzhen Weiwu was the Family Xiao's estate built by four brothers over ten years, completed in 1885.

In Southern China, many villages are called *zhen*, meaning gulley. The term *zhen* may be modified by an adjective to indicate its particular identity, for example, Shenzhen (a city next to Hong Kong). Dafu means big (*da*) belly (*fu*) to symbolise fertility A few years ago, *fu* was replaced by its homonym which means happiness.

The Dafuzhen gully is a series of man-made canals designed to supply and remove surface water from a hilly area down to the settlement and further to the agricultural land.

The Dafuzhen weiwu has been owned by the Xiao family for many generations. Over 130 years it has undergone repairs while retaining its original form intact. In 2012, decayed roof timbers and missing tiles were replaced. In 2013, Dafuzhen was listed as a provincial heritage by the Fujian government.

A brief account of the family history is given below, based on sources provided by the local heritage office and supplemented by our interview.

Dafuzhen was built in 1870 by four brothers, the third generation of the Xiao settled in Youxi. The Xiao was a farming family, who had engaged in the business of timber trading.

The grandfather, Xiao Hongwu, the ninth generation of the Xiao clan in Meixian (Youxi upstream) moved to this area and built a weiwu which still exists. The father, Xiao Shikuang had five consorts and each gave birth to a son. The eldest son did not join his brothers in building Dafuzhen. The relationship between them and the location of the eldest brother's house are not clear. For convenience, the four brothers are called 1 to 4 in this book. The social status of the Xiao was wealthy commoners, and the grade of their wealthy was modest. Dafuzhen is representative of traditional weiwu.

6. Dafuzhen is *c*. 300 m to Youxi Brook and 100 m to the old estate.
7. A raised pathway among the rice paddies leads to Dafuzhen at the foot of distant mountains.
8. An aerial shot of the Pingzai area in 2014 gives an idea of the environment. In the mid-ground is Dafuzhen, looking south.

9. The line of the Xiao family.
10. Xiao's old estate on a hill, completed in 1843, partially hidden from view by banana trees.
11. Gatehouse of Xiao's old compound facing East.
12. Structure of Xiao's old weiwu: a post-and-tie framework with bamboo-and-daub infill, and a raised wooden floor. Posts are slender, varying in height. Between every two posts there is a strut. All vertical members are interlocked by tie-beams, and each member supports a purlin, upon which rafters rest directly.

The line of the Xiao family

Xiao Hongwu (grandfather, 1778-1850)
built the old weiwu

Shipei | Shida | Shikuang (father) Stayed in the old

Liangsong | Liangbing | Liangyao | Liangxian | Liang'an

Weiwu unknown

Dafuzhen Weiwu

Dafuzhen residents and their lifestyle

The residents are the descendants of the four brothers. At its height, there were 36 families, about 168 people, of the Xiao clan at Dafuzhen. In the 1950s, the compound was used as a commune kitchen and village storage. In the late 1960s–1970s, Dafuzhen functioned as an evening school or a meeting place for the community. In the 1980s, the Xiao people returned to Dafuzhen. From the 1990s onwards, people moved out to new buildings. The population has decreased greatly since then, to about 25 inhabitants today.

13–15. Youngsters and seniors of Dafuzhen.
16. The residents are intensive agriculturalists.
17. Dafuzhen Headman in front of the estate. The frontage is finished with painting and writing survived from different periods of time.
18. Sister-in law of the headman drying homemade noodles on a bamboo panel.

13 14 15
16 17 18

Research methods and objectives

In China, if a date has to be put on the appearance of a modern scholarship on vernacular architecture it would be 1957. That year saw the publication of a book, *A Brief Introduction of Chinese Dwellings* by Liu Dunzhen. Since then, scholars have studied vernacular architecture with a number of objectives. The inhabited space and its daily use have been studied for social, cultural and ethnic information; the structures and forms have been documented for data acquisition thus architectural historiography.

This book is a case study about the Dafuzhen weiwu for two reasons: its architectural and planning sophistication as is immediately evident to us, and its commoners status. Our tasks are: first, to survey in situ each building part of the complex in the current situation with attention to details; second, to portray what are hidden from view with masterly »x-ray« eyes; third, to convey the information in measured drawings at technological and design levels.

Our work is graphic and analytical in nature, ranged within a series of research questions: What is the weiwu typologically and structurally? What was the planning made to suit the hillside

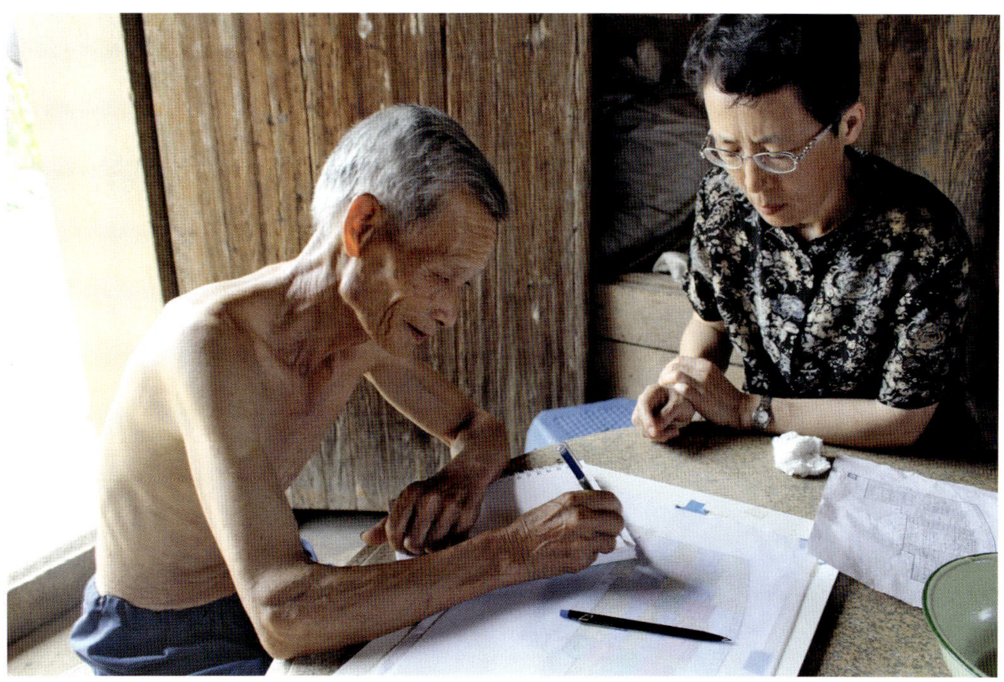

19. After two-year preparations, we returned to Dafuzhen in 2014 to carry out a research project with a group of students to document the complex inside and out, which forms the main body of this book.

20. Chinese has a textual tradition recording history. Xiao is a literate family, but after the wars, the family-books, if there were any that survived, have been lost since the cultural revolution (1966–1976). We use a variety of non-textual methods and sources, including on-site conversation with locals.

setting? What was the architectural arrangement made to accommodate the community living? To what extent do water supply and drainage design serve as a planning strategy? This study suggests that water management was a key issue which however was not a topic of great interest in traditional scholarship.

This book presents the physical structures of Dafuzhen with descriptive analysis in graphic form. The study interprets the architecture and planning based in the conjunctive approach. The objective of this study is to show not only its "as-built" condition, but also how to build. Decoration is not discussed in the book, but was touched on in the scope of the investigation.

21. A joint-teaching and research project was carried out by Qinghua Guo and Yuyu Chang. The team consisted of the third-year architectural students of Zhejiang University, Gunnar Almevik and Ross Berryman. Photo shows the team and the locals who prepared food for us three times a day for two weeks.

Architecture and planning

Zones and functions

Dafuzhen consists of five parts, a common area, living quarters, a private school, workshop and watchtowers.

A: common area with a central entrance (B, C, D & H: living quarters, each one with an entry, except H);
B: the elder brother's to the right of A (facing south);
C: the second brother's to the left (East);
D: the third brother's to the right beside B;
H: the youngest brother's to the right adjacent to D;
E, F: auxiliary buildings, privies next to F;
I: belonging to a later stage in the development, by which time privies were filled in, resulting in the asymmetrical layout of the complex today. The encircled walls contain small exits on both sides, i.e., east and west.
K: watchtower. There were three, and all were demolished in the late 1950s. Two were rebuilt in the 1990s (K1 and K2);
G & J: private (or family) school;
L: workshop (later used as a stable for livestock).

Dafuzhen is now punctuated by four modern buildings built prior to 2010 within or immediately next to it.

1. Dafuzhen plan.
2. In front of the common area of zone A, there is an open ground of a rectangular and a half circular in plan. The rectangular space is a »lobby« at the main entrance to the compound, and the half circular was originally a pond formed due to digging out clay for building construction.

3. Open and shared spaces.

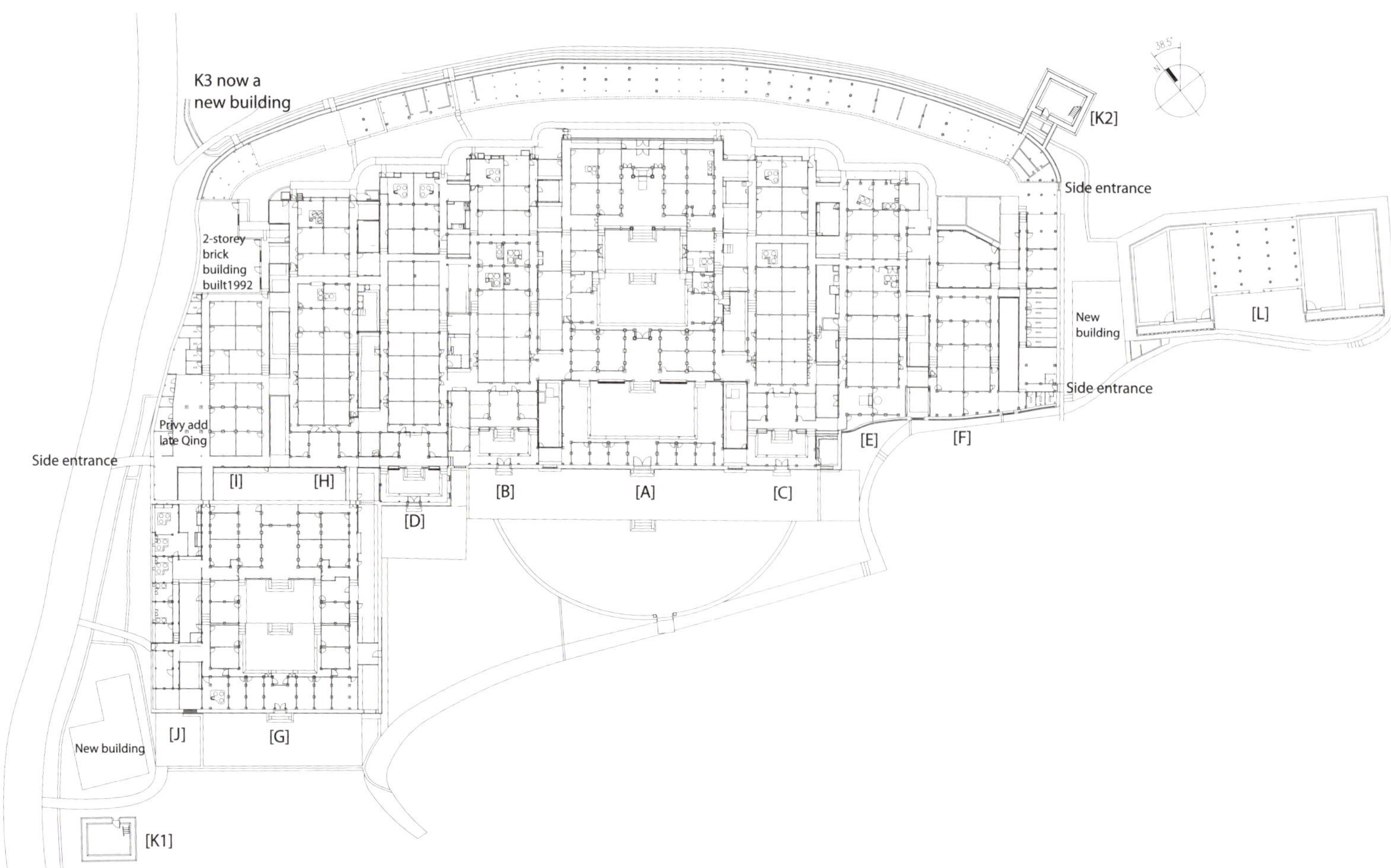

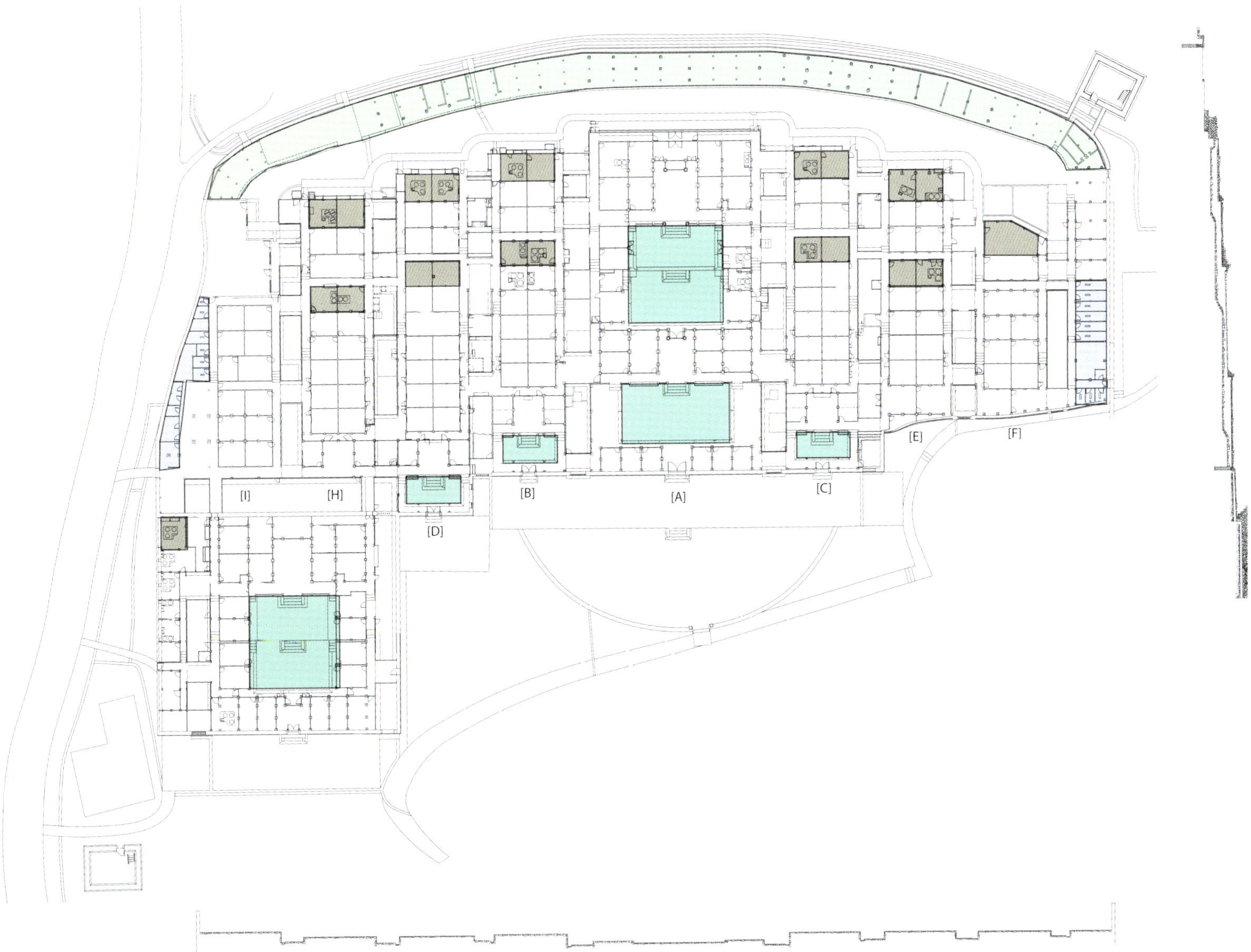

Kitchen and roofed vent

Privy and woodshed

Courtyard with entrance
Longhouses of B, C and D, each has a front yard with an entrance which reveal that they are facing the society as equal units of the family.

E: subfamily rooms
F and I: accommodating guests

Site and planning

Dafuzhen is 5974 sq. m in size, and the building area is 3600 sq. m (N–S 68 m, E–W 114 m). The site flows up the slope via terraces upon which buildings are erected. The terraced area (excluding the school) stepped in four levels is N–S 36.8 m in length. The level difference between front and rear is 3.4 m, having an average grade of 5.3 percent. Controlling water is essential to life and crops. Water flows to the site through eight canals, each 2.8 m wide and 0.8 m deep in average. The canals are stepped and sloped, carrying water flowing at a certain rate and preventing washout after excessive rainfall.

4. Terraced site and drainage network.

5. Size and layout.

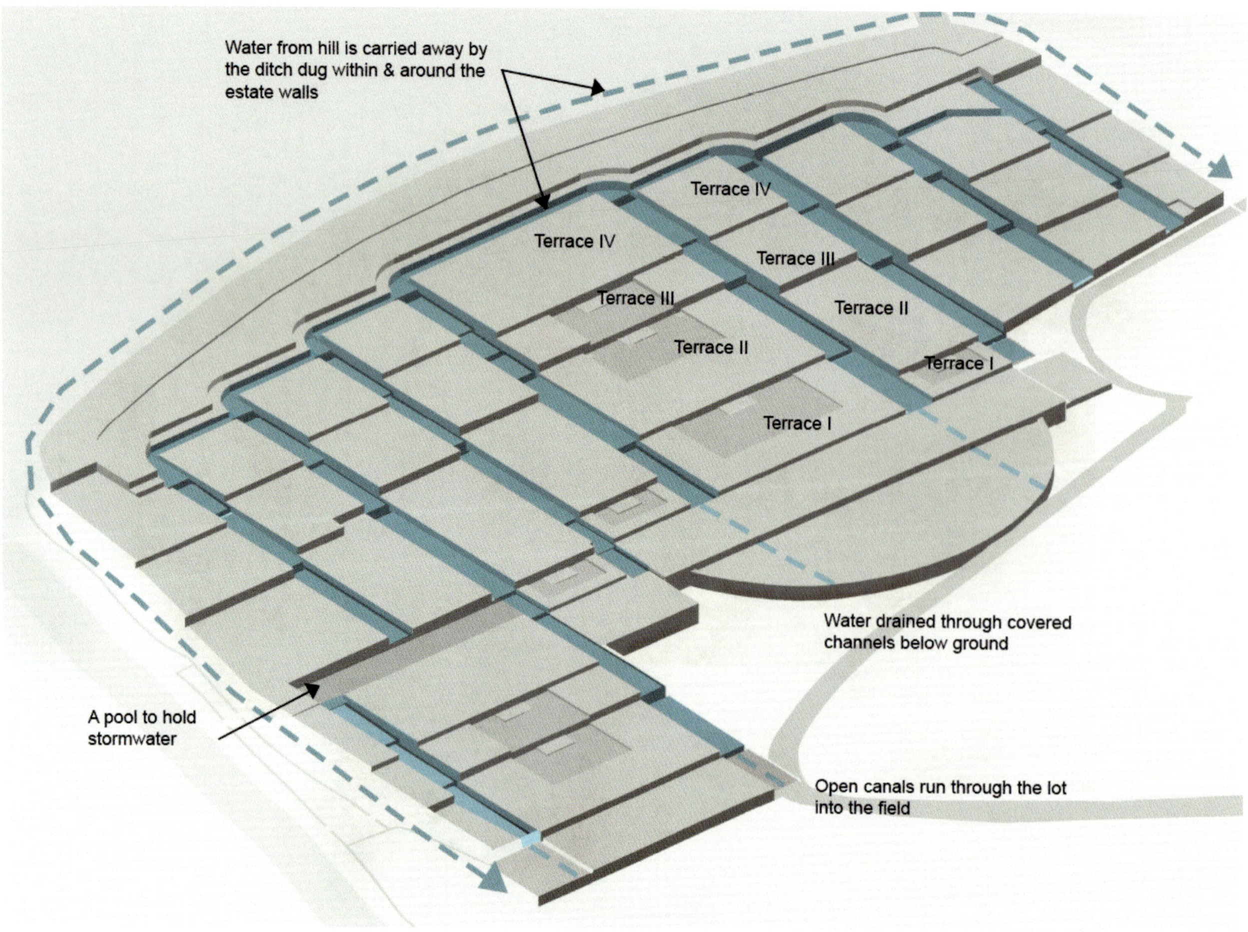

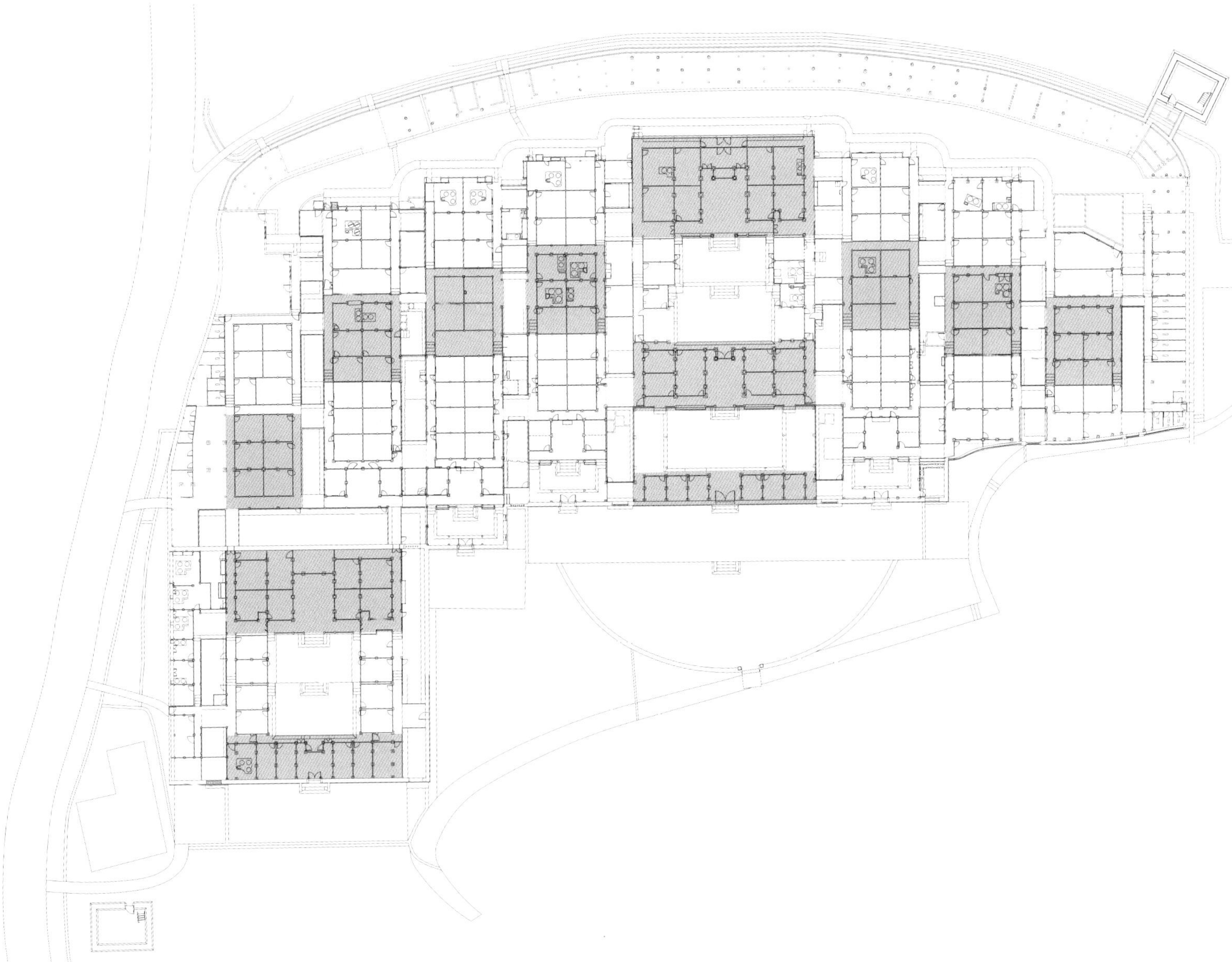

Size, type and layout

Dafuzhen is a formal compact compound on a rural hillside setting. Its common area is positioned in the centre with longhouses on both sides. Two building types in terms of planning are identified: courtyard and longhouse. The two are carefully laid out in proportion with each other. There is a visual rhythm created by the longhouses repeated regularly and symmetrically.

The length of longhouses is largely 3 bays, a few 4 and 2 bays, and one 5 bays. All are 2 bays in width. The 3-bay seems to be a basic unit in planning. We understand that a defined unit of measurement was employed in building and planning, thus proportions were determined.

Longhouses
3 x 2 bay
4 x 2 bay
5 x 2 bay
2 x 2 bay

Courtyard housing
5 x 2 bay
5 x 1 bay

Gridiron plan

6. Gridiron plan.

It is observed that there is a geometric symmetry in the layout of houses and a gridiron plan for Dafuzhen. The grid is made up of integrated longhouses and canals. This suggests that there existed projected units of measurement repeated consistently in architecture and planning. In other words, the measurements are a notation system based upon repeated units which have a mathematical and physical reality.

In our measured drawings all measurements are in the metric system instead of the traditional system (which was used originally). As modularity exists in Dafuzhen design, this creates no analytical difficulty.

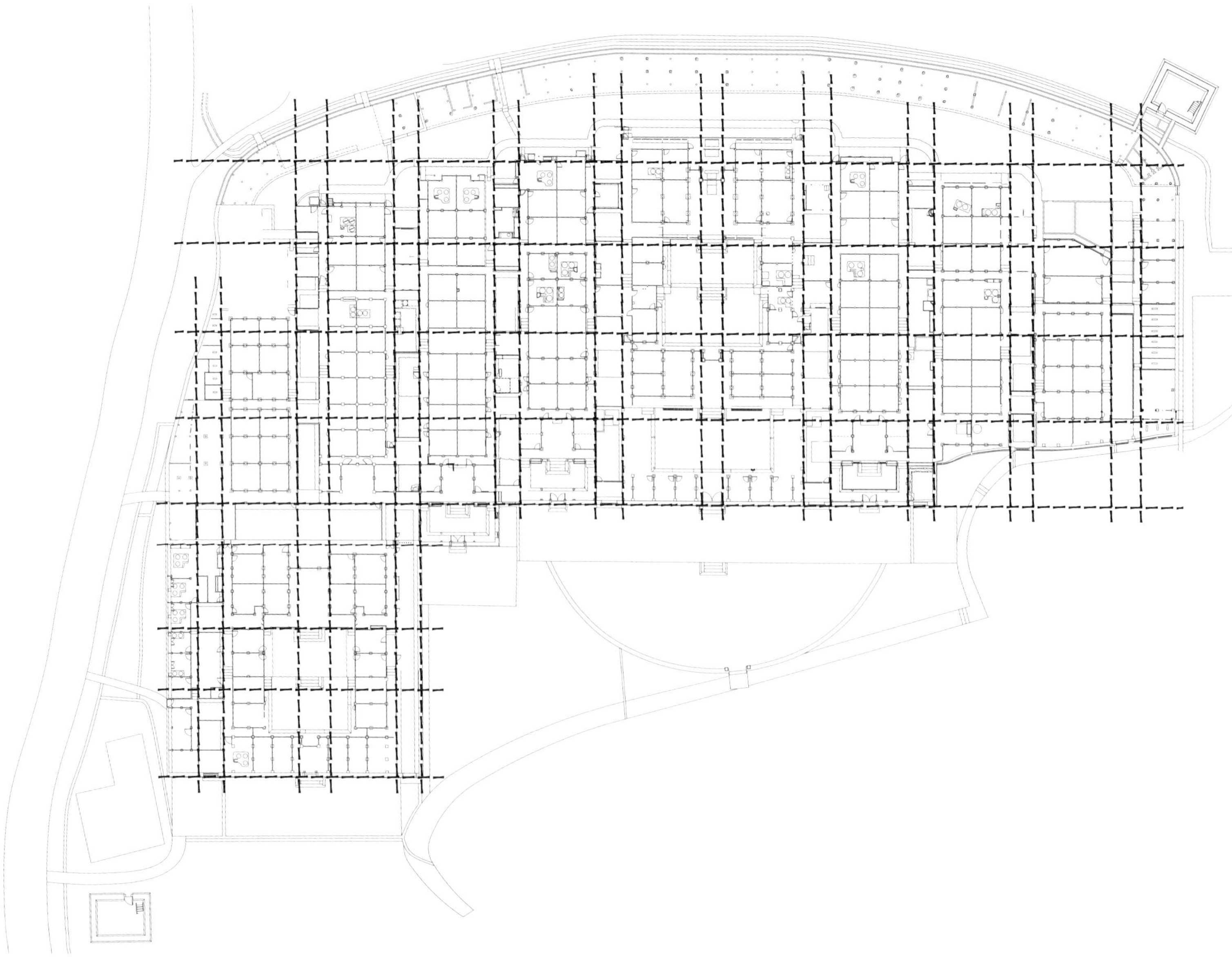

7. Simplified layout of Dafuzhen.

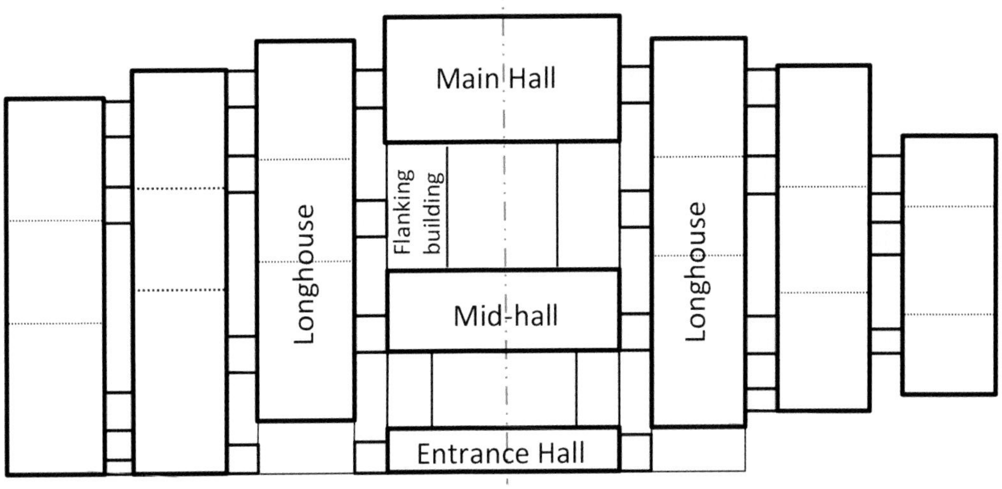

Typology and development

The weiwu has two main components: a common area and a private quarter. They are clearly distinct in architectural orientation and spatial organisation and are arranged with careful regard to symmetry.

The common area is a type of courtyard architecture formed by three longitudinal halls and two courtyards arranged in an ordered sequence in the middle as a nucleus of the compound. There is a visual centre and an imaginary straight line that goes through the centre and divides the compound into two equal halves. The private quarter consists of three longhouses transversely arranged on each side in rows, three buildings a row.

Dafuzhen is a planned compound which reveals a rational utilisation of organisation principles. This is an ordered environment, where Confucianism provides moral principles. Architectural order and spatial sequence are consistent with the moral order.

Typological genesis

Our typological study shows that the buildings in the common area belong to the courtyard architecture and the buildings in the living quarters are reminiscent of longhouses. That is, Dafuzhen connects to two distinctive types of architecture – courtyard housing and longhouse. They have an ancient history: the longhouse has Southern antecedents and represents the earliest form of permanent structure. The courtyard housing is the northern phenomenon, and the oldest way of grouping buildings. Dafuzhen weiwu, in essence, is a combination of both to suit new, migrant purposes.

Tracking down the origin of the weiwu

Dafuzhen does not reflect the evolution of architecture from a single source. Courtyard housing and longhouses might both have shaped the practice of weiwu. Courtyard housing is a compound with buildings surrounding a courtyard on all sides, which is one of the most ancient housing patterns, dating back to three thousand years ago.

Zone A and zone G have traits of courtyard architecture represented, for instance, by that now existing in Dingcun, Shanxi province. The Dingcun courtyard housing is multi-courtyard. The building was erected on a platform with an entrance on the long side.

The buildings in the private quarter belong to a type of longhouses which has been a historical heritage deeply rooted to Chinese traditions and culture.

In comparison to the ancient courtyard architecture and longhouses, Dafuzhen bears a strong resemblance to both forms in design and planning, which may be attributed to the dispersal of peoples and their transporting of building types and technologies with them which they adopted.

The weiwu is the outcome of a long tradition of received techniques, or assembling by experimentation, or based on detailed calculations or formulae (see page 110).

In a diffusionist perspective, the weiwu is a hybrid phenomenon or new innovation. Such architectural diffusions may have been in a scale and span far greater than that once believed.

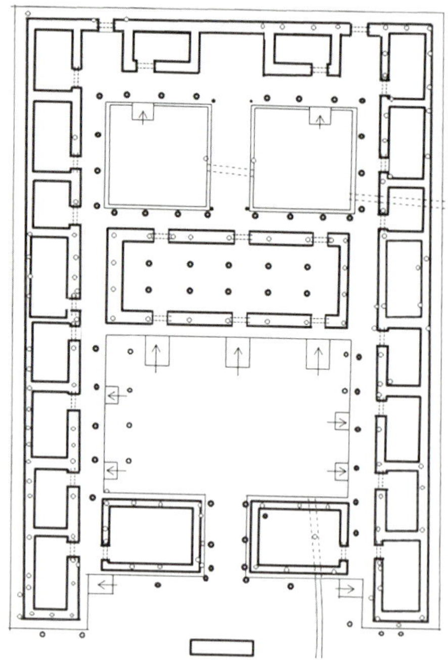

Typological development

Historical sources and architectural evidences enable us to interpret that the weiwu's overall design is indebted to courtyard housing and longhouses. But, we are unable to tell when the two were merged and developed into a particular type. One thing is certain: Weiwu was a distinguished type of domestic architecture of the Ming–Qing period primarily in Fujian.

Weiwu development was probably driven by population and directly related to topography. The appearances of weiwu vary, but the principle remains unchanged. The primary reason for the persistence and spread of weiwu was that it reached a level of perfection to satisfy family structure and property security.

Dafuzhen consists of two courtyards and six longhouses. The canal design allows the longhouses to be juxtaposed. The resulting higher density provides for economy of construction. The canals are indispensable parts of the architectural ensembles of the weiwu.

8. Courtyard housing in Beijing (Ming-Qing period). It is a multi-courtyard complex with a garden. The buildings are single storeyed, arranged on four sides to form a courtyard arranged in sequence.
9. The most eminent example of Neolithic longhouses is at Yuchisi site in Mengcheng, Anhui province. For example, house no. 5, consisting of 10 rooms, were built with wattle and daub in wooden frames.
10. Courtyard compound of Western Zhou (1046 to 771 BC). Its main building is 6-bay wide and 3-bay deep facing south. After *Wenwu*, 1979, 10, fig. 4.

11. Typological development through time.

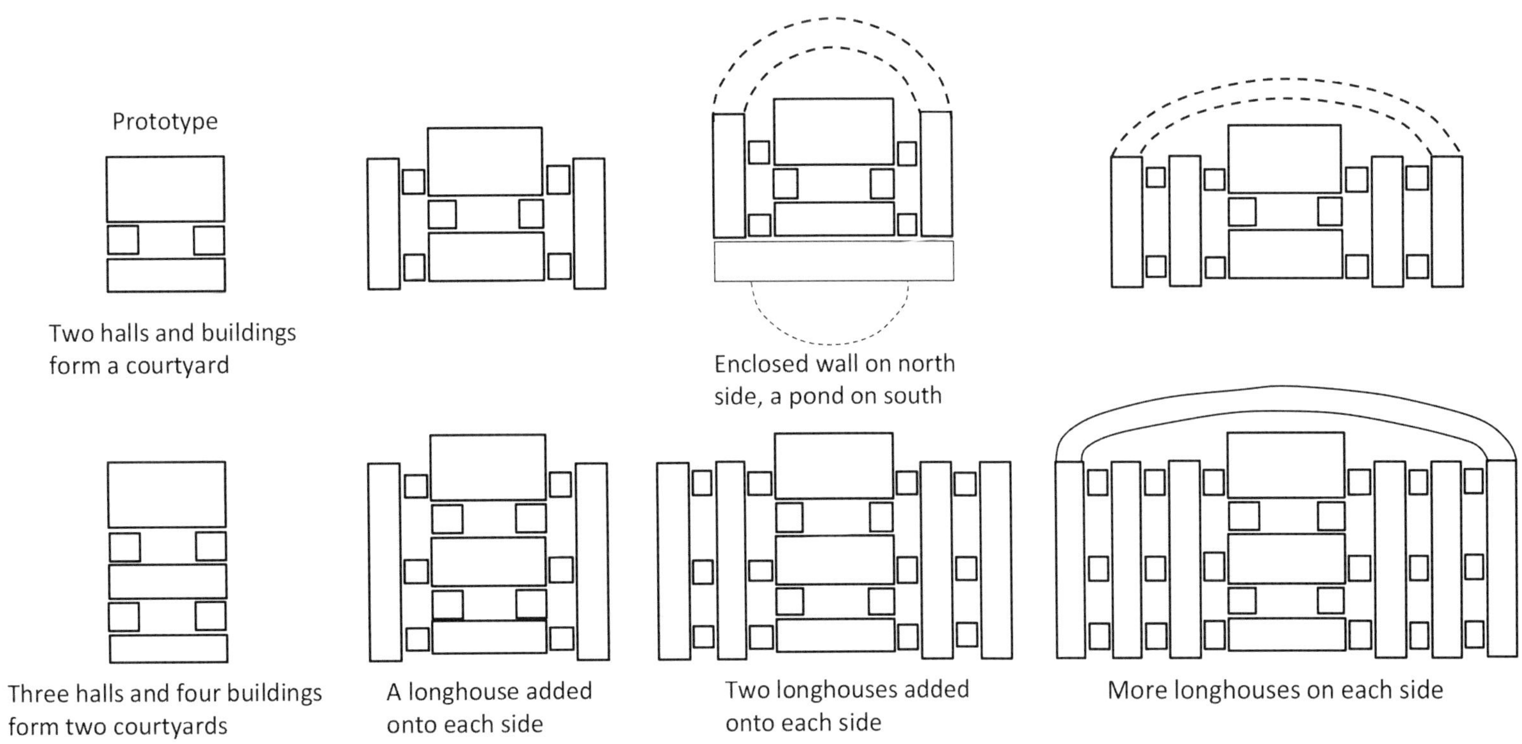

Courtyard architecture

Common area, zone A

The central zone is formal courtyard architecture having two open spaces arranged one behind the other. The second courtyard consists of two levels.

The buildings along the axis employ the strongest contract of heights and decorations. The central bay of B1 functions as an entrance hall; that of B2 is a middle hall and that of B3 is a main hall. Located on a platform, B3 is the largest and tallest building in the compound. Its transverse frameworks are asymmetrical – the rear half is greater than the front in depth.

The exterior of Dafuzhen is enclosed, solid and hard; the interior is open, framed and soft. The heart of the compound and the focus of all its life is the courtyard. In hot summer, people escape the heat by retreating to well-ventilated halls and porches; in other times, they enjoy the sun in the open living space.

12. Section through the central bays.
13. Courtyard architecture is bigger than others.

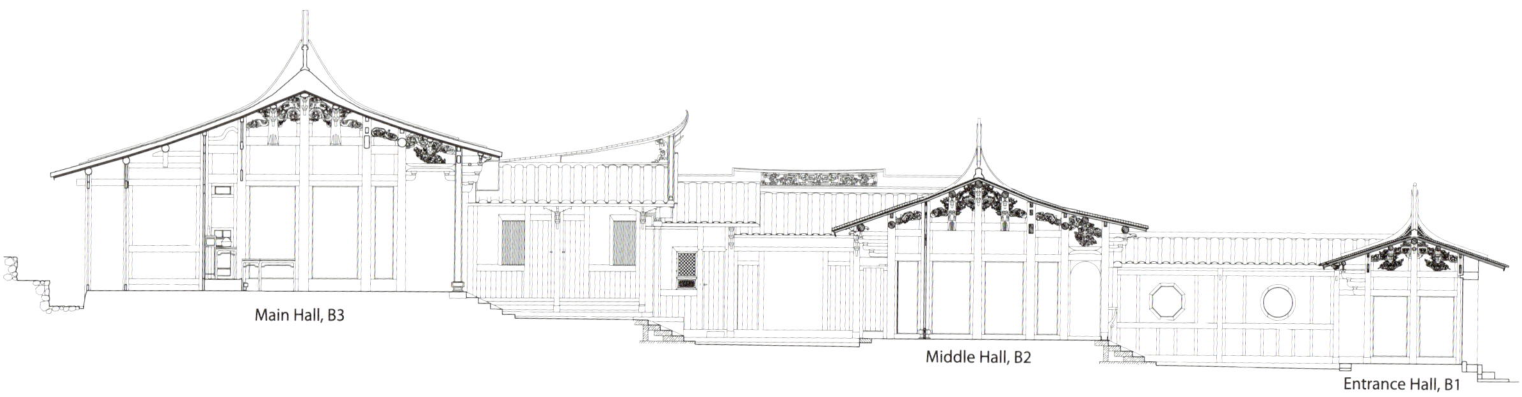

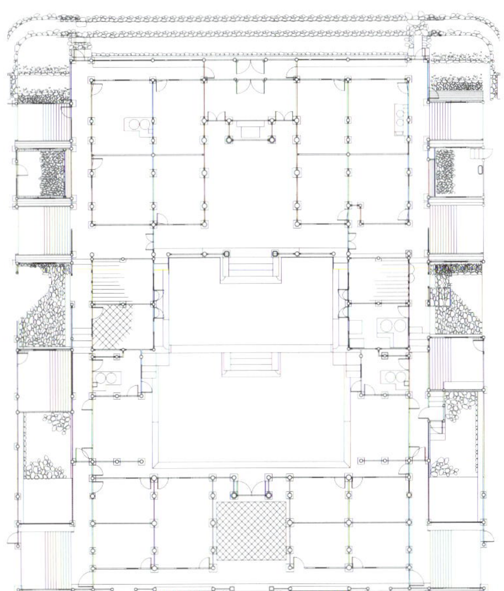

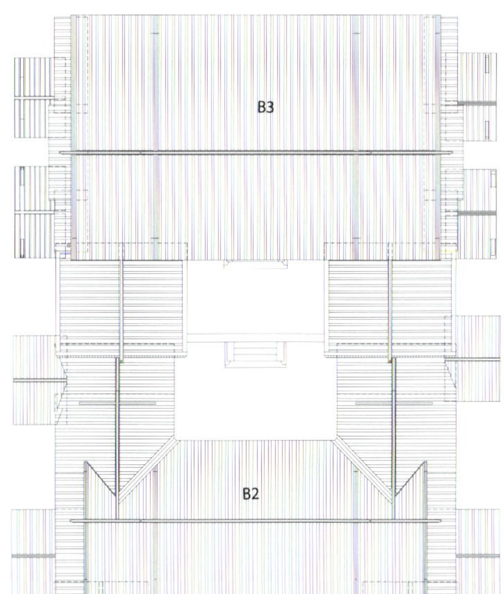

14 17
15
16 18
19 20

14. Courtyard 1, a principle open space.
15. The main hall is erected on a platform which gives the building a grand appearance.
16. Front elevation of the east flanking building.
17. Entrance to the central zone.
18. Middle Hall, view through to the main hall. The double-door in the middle is only open on special occasions.
19. Roof plan.
20. Floor plan.

Main hall

The main hall is 5 by 2-bay (20.5 x 10.8 m) in plan. The bay-widths do not reduce from the centre towards the end, which is due to correspondence between the end-bay of the main hall and that of the flanking building.

The central bay is open-fronted, and bigger than the others, containing a built-in alcove for ancestral tablets. On the anniversaries, the tablets are displayed, and offerings are perched on tables. Ancestral rituals, wedding and birthday celebrations, death ceremonies and feasts take place in the hall, which is the most elaborately decorated room in the estate. The rooms accompanying the central bay are reserved for respected elders. There is a small chamber hiding behind the partition at the back. The central hall is 5.3 x5.8 m and the rear chamber is 5.3 x 2.3 m in plan.The rear room hidden from view is a coffin chamber, opened only on ceremonial occasions. The deceased would be moved into the coffin chamber from the back door but departed through the west door of the central hall according to traditional customs.

21. The main hall is a single-storeyed building: its central bay is full-height; its side- and end-bay has a mezzanine constructed above the ground floor. Section through the end-bay.
22. The veranda is enclosed by latticed panels across the rear side, Main hall.

23. Mezzanine, main hall.
24. Rear elevation, the main hall is treated as three portions in terms of roof design.
25. The main-hall plan

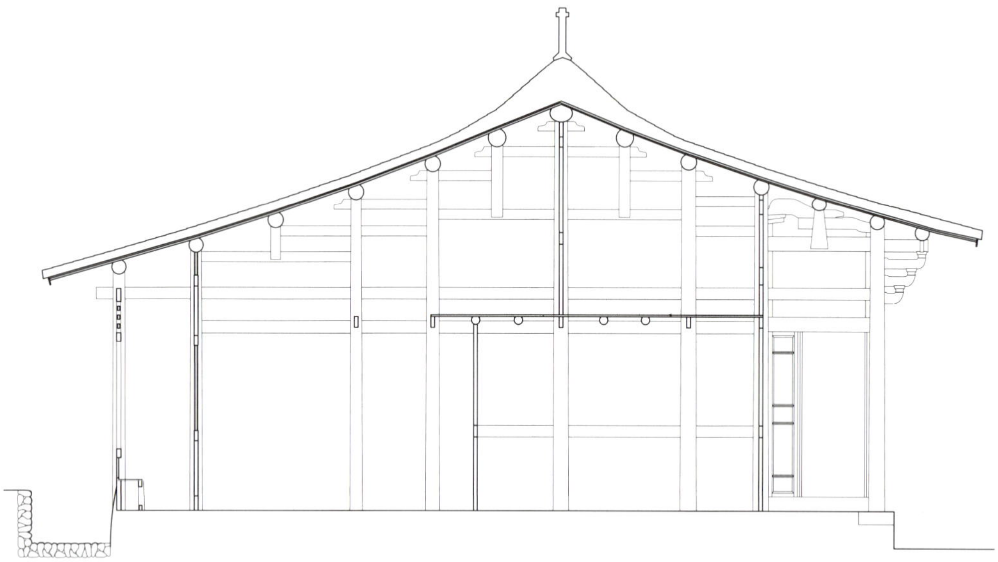

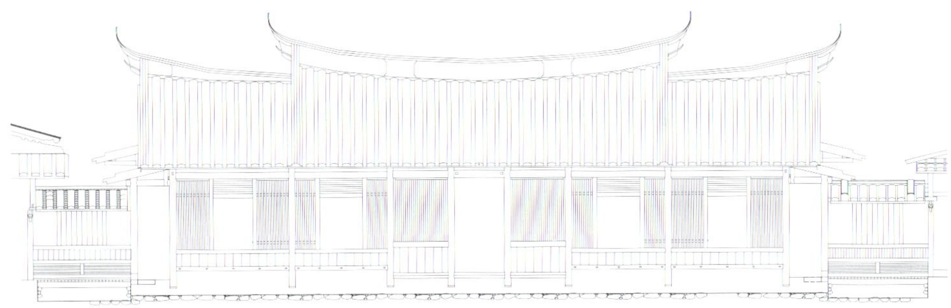

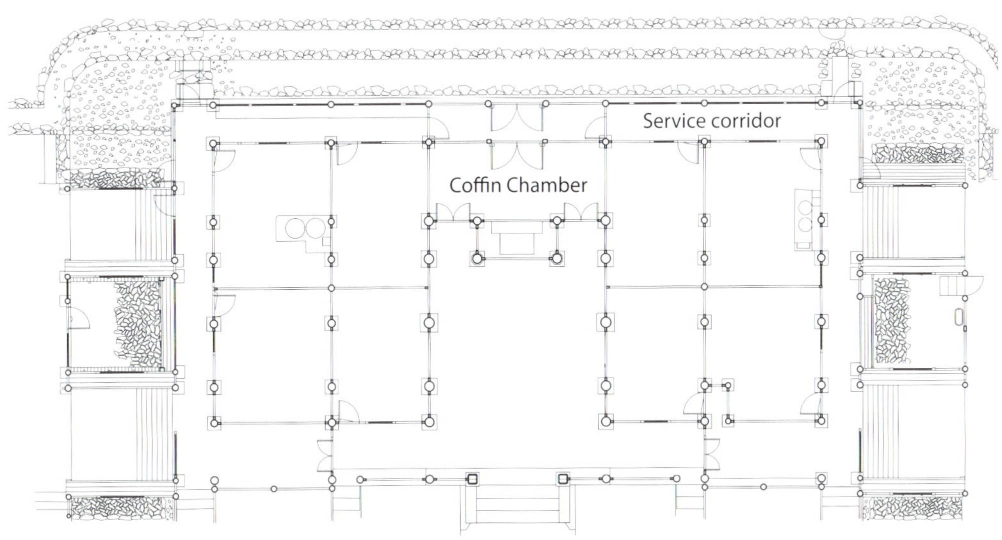
Service corridor
Coffin Chamber

Private school, zone G

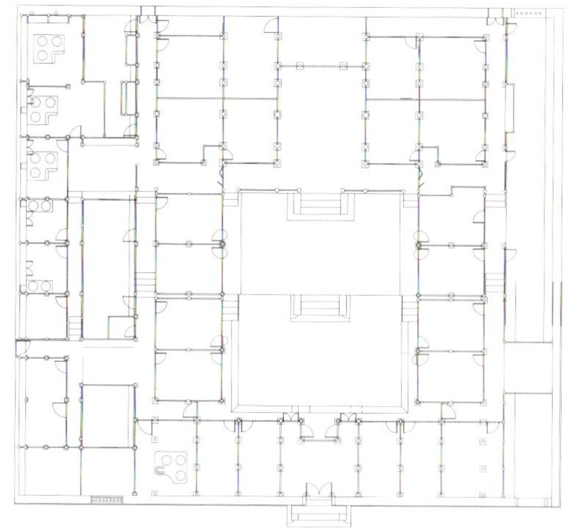

Located in front and to the west of the estate, the school is courtyard architecture with an open space in two levels. In terms of layout, architecture and structure, it is a replica of the second courtyard of zone A.

In the old time, the lecture hall was used for teaching the children of Family Xiao. Some rooms were used for accommodating teachers. The longhouse behind the courtyard, to the west, provided service spaces. The school area is 28.5 x 26 m, total 740 sq. m.

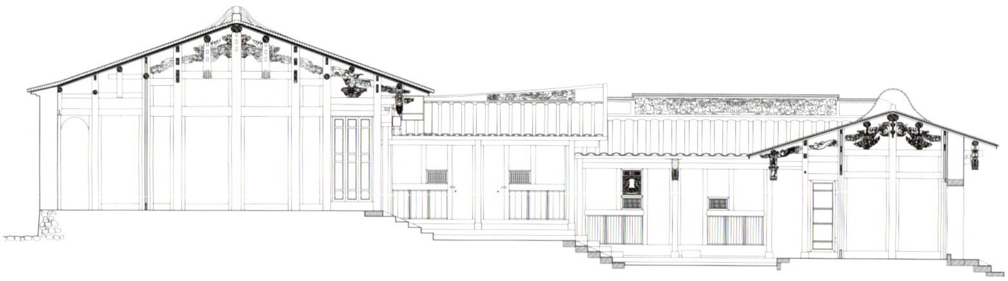

26. Section through the central bays of Lecture Hall and Entrance Hall, School.
27. School viewed from above.
28. School floor plan.

29. View from the lecture hall to the entryway.
30. Lecture Hall. The slogans on the wall were written in the late 1960s when it was a village meeting place. The building is formed by transverse and longitudinal frameworks, as we shall see later in Erection process.

Gable roof, overlapping eaves and eaves in gable wall

The lecture hall is much bigger than the entrance hall in depth and height. Between the two halls are two flanking buildings on each side. The buildings are the same in size but located on two different ground levels. The entrance hall and its adjacent flanking buildings are the same in size and height.

31. Eaves are added symmetrically in the gable wall. East elevation, lecture hall.
32, 34. The flanking building's gable wall is under and covered by the main hall's eaves. The photographs show two examples with different details: the gaps between the gable wall and the eaves are visible (right), and the other concealed (left). The gable framework of the latter is elaborate, that of the former is simple.
33. Roof plan, School. The main hall is double-sloping roofed, with a gable wall at both ends. The main hall and flanking buildings are of different sizes. The former is much bigger and taller than the latter. Their roofs are therefore partially overlapping.

35. Common area, zone A.
36. Private school, zone G.

Similarities and differences of the courtyard architecture

The main halls of zone A and zone G are similar in principle, and vary in details. Noticeably, the roof ridge of A is significantlyupward curving whereas that of G is slightly upward curving.

Front elevation

East elevation

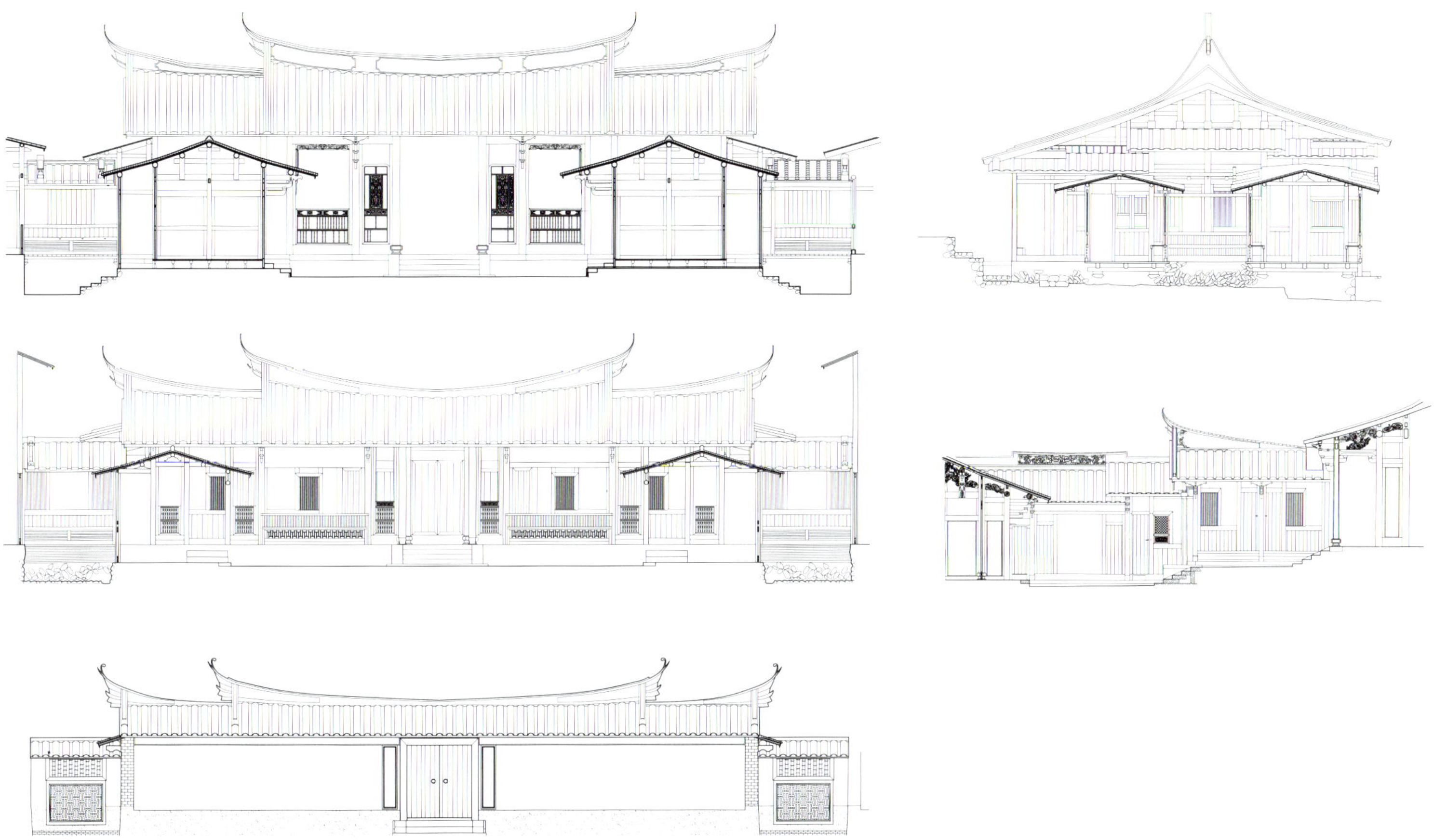

Main hall

Middle hall

Entrance hall

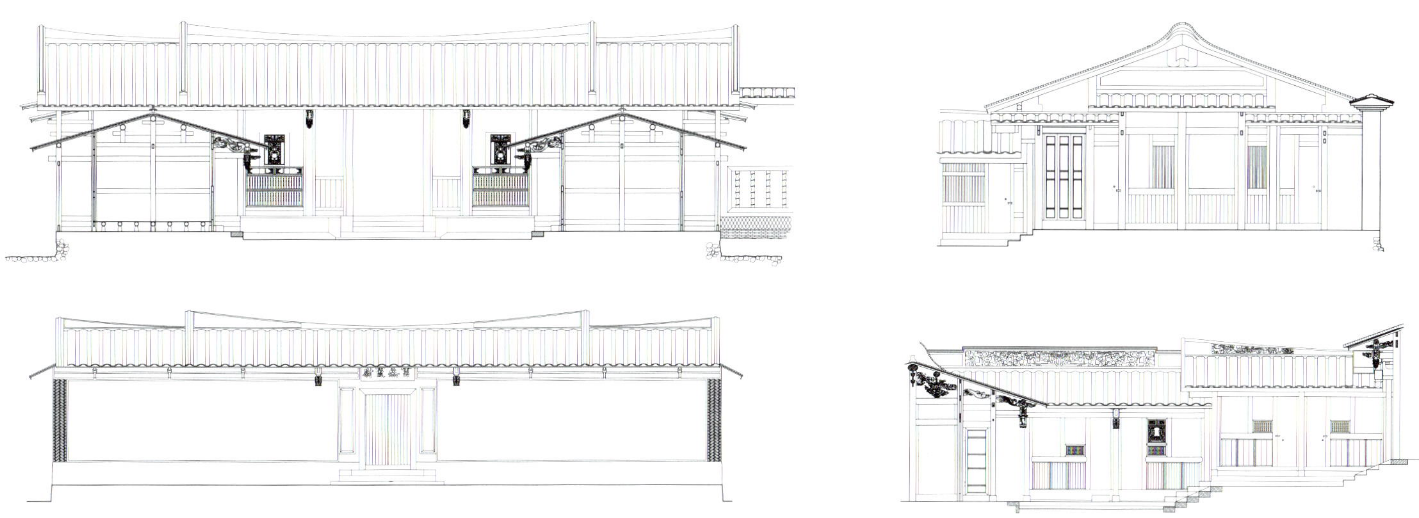

Main hall

Entrance hall

Wooden carving

In the main hall, carving is made between posts under the roof. The load-bearing members do not bear decoration. Details and degree of ornamentations vary from main hall to main hall.

37. Richly carved ornamentation representing plants twining round trees, main hall, zone A.
38. Stylised plants of infinite variety used for enriching flat surfaces, carved in relief. Entrance Hall, zone G.
39. Finely carved members decorating the foyer of the main hall, zone A.

40. Recurving plants surround a landscape painting. Building D.
41. A series of painting disposed alternately with calligraphy in a row under the eaves, zone A.

Wall painting

The frontage of the estate is decorated, particularly the upper portion of the wall, with brush painting and calligraphy on the mud plaster. The painting covers several categories: landscape, flower-and-bird, and figure. The themes include Twenty-four Paragons of Filial Piety and Tale of the White Snake. Such paintings were indications of the Confucianist attitude of the master of the weiwu.

Living quarters: longhouses

The private zone consists of brothers' dwellings. In detail, on each side of the central zone, three or four longhouses are lining up north–south in parallel rows. Between them are canals. The longhouse is elevated on a series of terraces that are interconnected by steps. The building is designed with a veranda, porch and corridor along its perimeter and across its interior. They form a crisscross network to allow both longitudinal routes and transverse accesses.

42. Longhouses of I, H, D and B from left to right.
43. Veranda runs the entire length of a longhouse. Longhouse H.
44. Interior passageway providing access from one building to another.
45. Corridor along the compound wall connecting longhouses.

46. Intermediate space.

Intermediate space

The circulation of the compound is transacted by verandas, corridors, bridges, entryways / exits.

Verandas, porches, corridors

Over-canal roofed bridges (total 42)

Entryways (7) /exits (3)

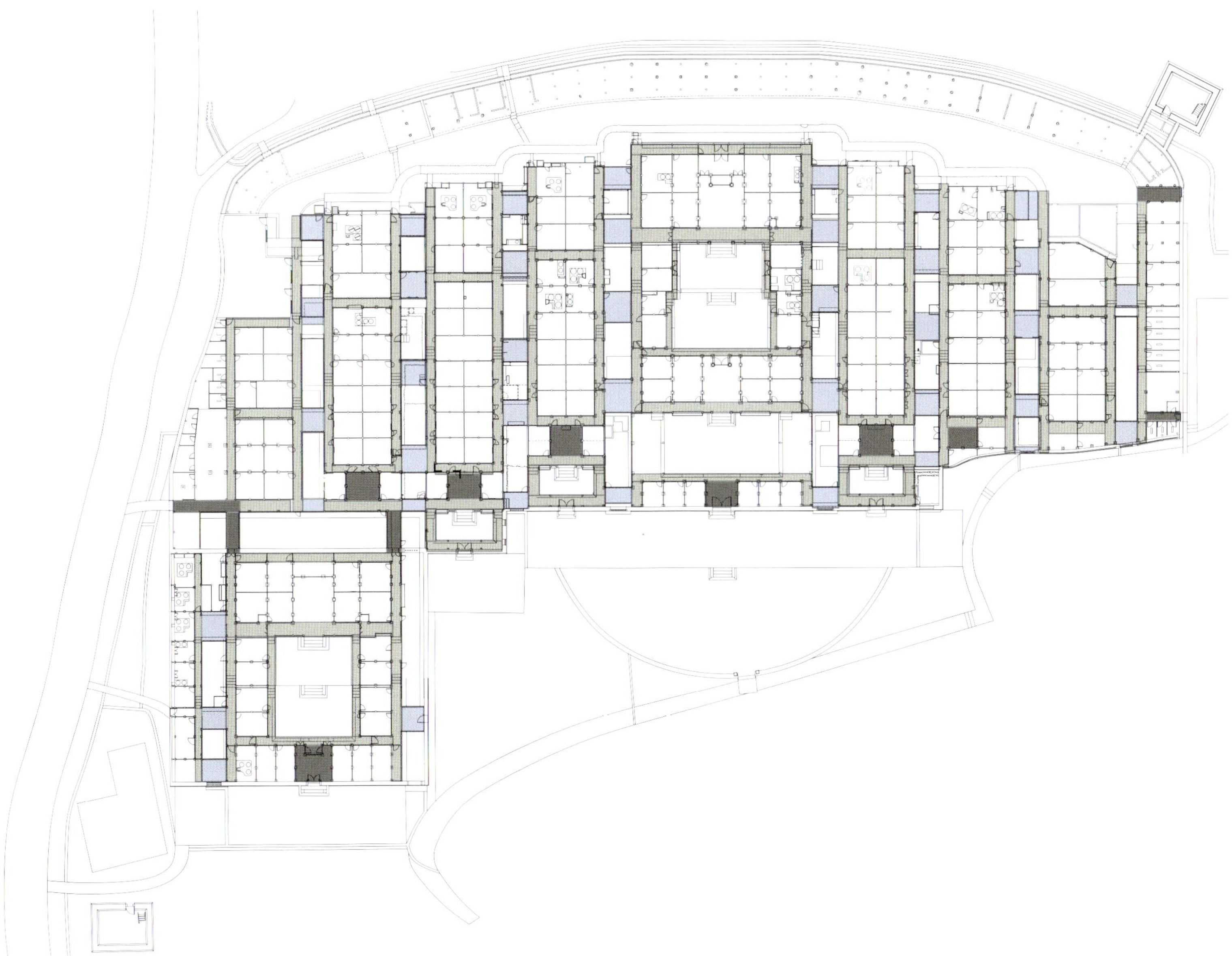

47. Connecting corridor in B1. A flexible spatial arrangement is achieved by adding partition walls in the framework.
48. B1 and B2 is one framework built on two terraces and covered by separate roofs.
49. Roofs of B2 and B3 overlap each other. B3 is not structurally connected to B2.

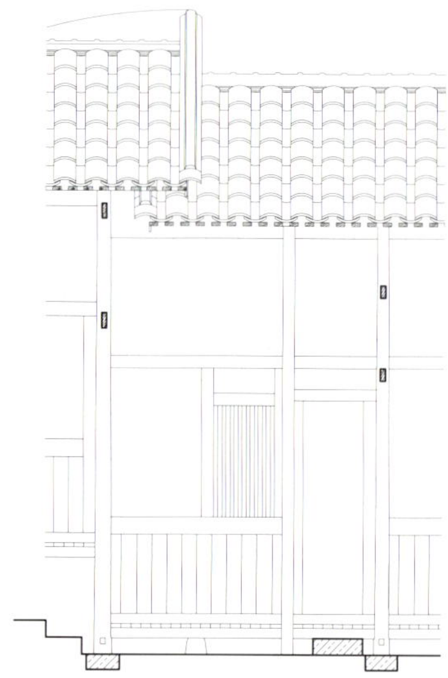

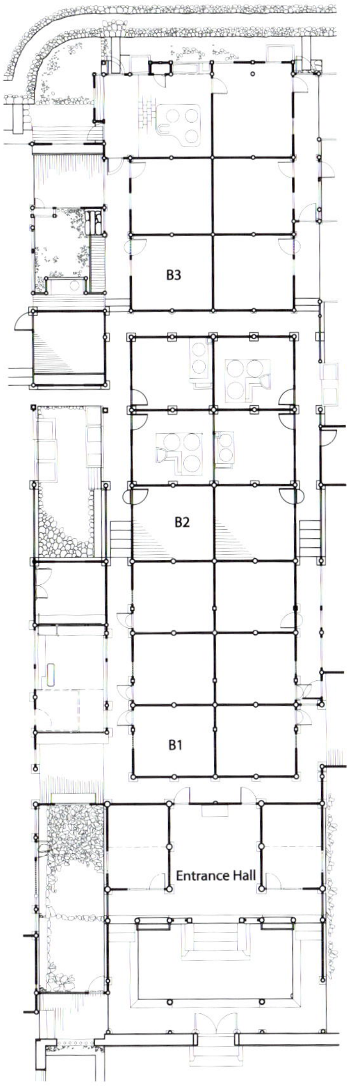

Longhouse B: first brother's

Built on four terraces, the longhouse consists of two similar structures (Building 1 and B2, B3) in a row. They were constructed with raised floors and covered by tiled roofs. B1 and B2 are distinguished as two buildings by roofs and terraces, but not by post-and-beam frameworks.

Symmetric in plan, the main entrance is on the short side at the lower end, and the kitchen at the rear end. The front building (B1) is 4-bay deep; the middle building (B2) is 3-bay deep, and the rear building (B3) is also 3-bay deep. All are 2-bay wide. The encircling verandas border the buildings to connect all dwelling units.

The 3-bay building consists of one earthen floor and two wooden floors. The 4-bay building consists of a 3-bay structure and an entrance. The entrance hall, facing the front yard and the entryway, has many different functions such as living room and reception room. The room on each side of it is a main bedroom.

Plan: 37.7 x 8.6 m
B1: 12.8 x 8.58 m (room or bay: 2.8 x 3.3 m, c. 9.2 sq. m)
B2: 9.65 x 8.58 (room: 2.9 x 3.3 m, c. 9.6 sq. m)
B3: 9.66 x 8.58 (room: 3 x 3.3 m, c. 9.8 sq. m)
Veranda: 1.03 m (wide); canal: 2.87 m (wide)

20 rooms in longhouse B used as kitchens, bedrooms and storages. The best rooms are facing the foreyard. Throughout history, the family compositions change, which alters the functions of some units.

Building 1 and Building 2 are covered by separated roofs. Structurally, they are one entirety, built on two levels. That is, the post-and-beam structure allows considerable flexibility in terms of spatial arrangement, such as creating two distinct spaces on different levels in a framework.

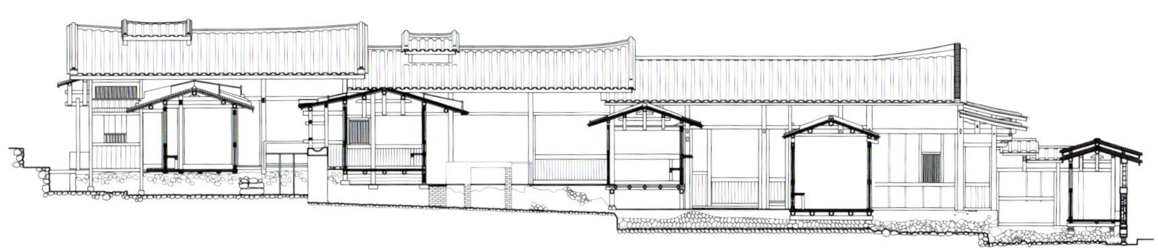

50. Floor plan, longhouse B.
51. Longhouse B.
52. Longhouse E.
53. Longhouse F.

Elevated-platform building vs raised-floor building

The entrance hall of a longhouse was erected on a platform and the living quarter behind was built with a raised floor of wooden planks. The construction of these two types of buildings differs on the basis of their flooring. This study claims that the longhouse consists of two types of buildings that belong to different lineages.

The terrace was coated in with a mixture of earth, lime and sand, which is rainproof. Floors of access and circulation spaces were finely smoothed. Posts rest on blocks of stone. Wooden floors are raised about 20 cm above the ground for purposes of air circulation. Dwelling units are enclosed by timber plank walls.

54. From the entrance hall view the living quarter, longhouse C.

55. View the entrance hall through the courtyard door, longhouse C.
56. Foreyard of longhouse D (similar to B and C). Stone slabs are used along platform edges and as steps, precisely finished. The courtyard is surfaced with fine plaster.
57. View the long side of longhouse D (B1 and B2) and the short side.
58. Floor boards are connected by half-lap joints.

55
56 57 58

59. Curtain down means »do not disturb«, longhouse B.

60. Dwelling unit is small, equipped with a window. Longhouse C.

61. Screened veranda, longhouse C.

Bedroom: The plank-floored rooms are sleeping rooms. The floor was designed to keep moisture out and to allow air circulation. Inside, the bedroom is furnished with a couch, table and wardrobe.

Footstep stone: The wooden floor is raised up and a half-circular stone is provided as a step in front of a door. The footstep is a place for taking off one's shoes before entering a bedroom. The stone marks the entry and the indoor / outdoor boundary.

Curtain: It is customary to hang a curtain from a door header. The curtain is a divider to screen off a private room and also serves as a sign – to pull it down is remind everyone who walks by that the people inside do not want to be interrupted at this time.

Latticed screen and visual privacy: The veranda of a longhouse is enclosed by a board fence and screened by a latticed framework, one above the other. The lattice framework is constructed of bars that are spaced vertically and fitted into the top and bottom rails. They serve as screens to let through air and provide shade. The latticework also creates a soft boundary between adjacent longhouses to prevent being seen into.

Longhouses of B, C, D, E, F, H and I

This page and the opposite page list elevations of all longhouses showing standardised design. The south elevations' main feature is a three-portioned porch against the gable wall; the north elevations' notable feature is high windows above the overhang eaves.

Entrances to longhouses of B and D are not totally identical, as the former's opening is framed and the latter's is arched.

I H D

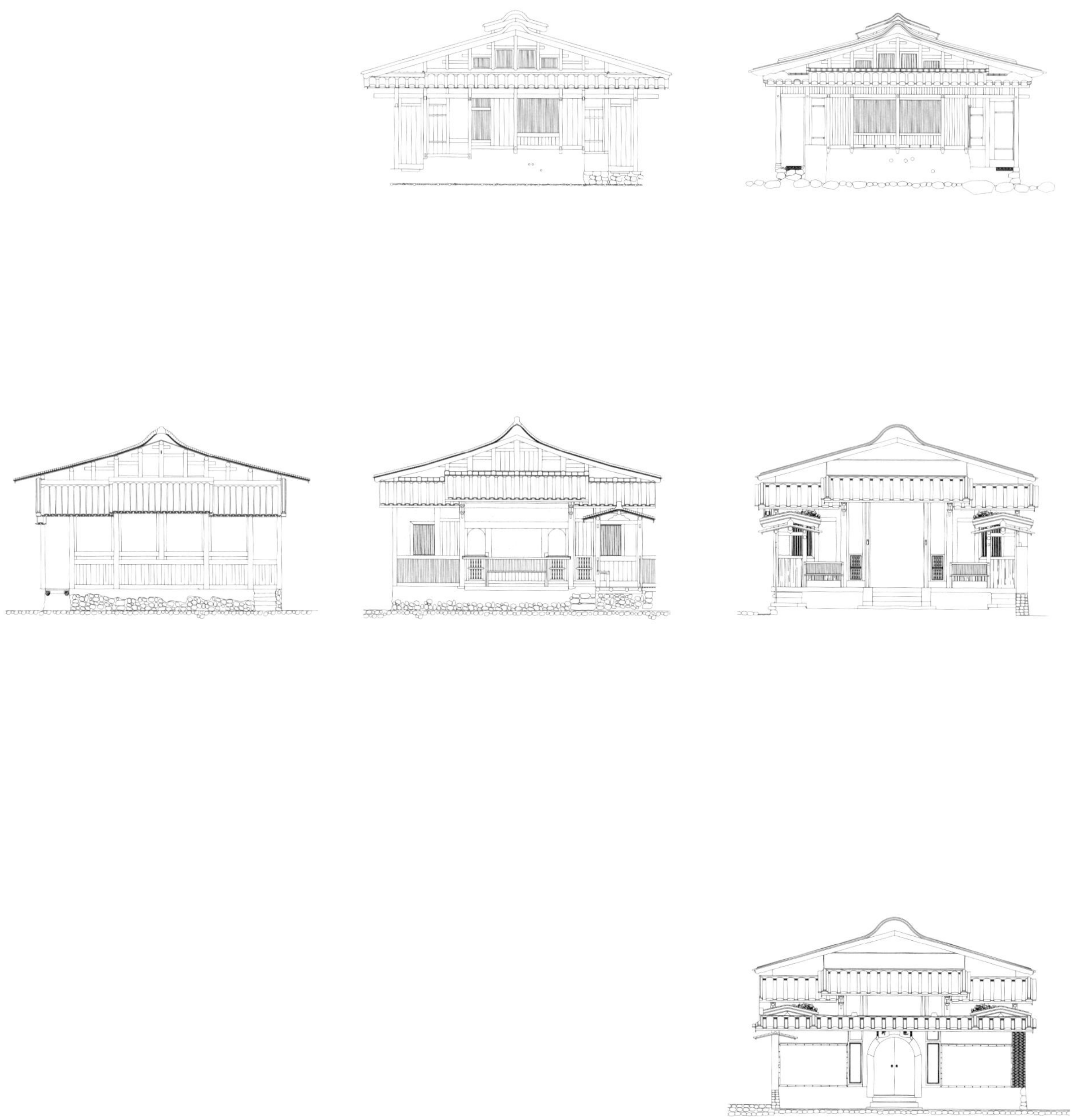

62. South, north and entrance elevations of long-houses.

Typology, prefabrication and standardisation

The weiwu is a timber-framed structures constructed on the post-and-beam principle. This type of structures is termed *Chuandou*, common in south China. Posts are used at intervals of 2 m or so, with intermediate struts. They are tied together by tie-beams in various arrangements to form transverse frameworks, and the frameworks, in turn, are connected by purlins rested on the posts and struts to form a building.

The sections of Dafuzhen buildings reveal the rational ordering of frameworks: the longhouse is symmetrical; the main hall is not – the rear half is greater than the front half in depth, a way to increase the building size while retaining the front-eaves height.

The timber buildings were prefabricated and assembled. The assemblies were standardised members manufactured in the workshop. The standardisations ensure the buildings to be successfully erected on site.

63. Structural paradigm of Dafuzhen buildings.

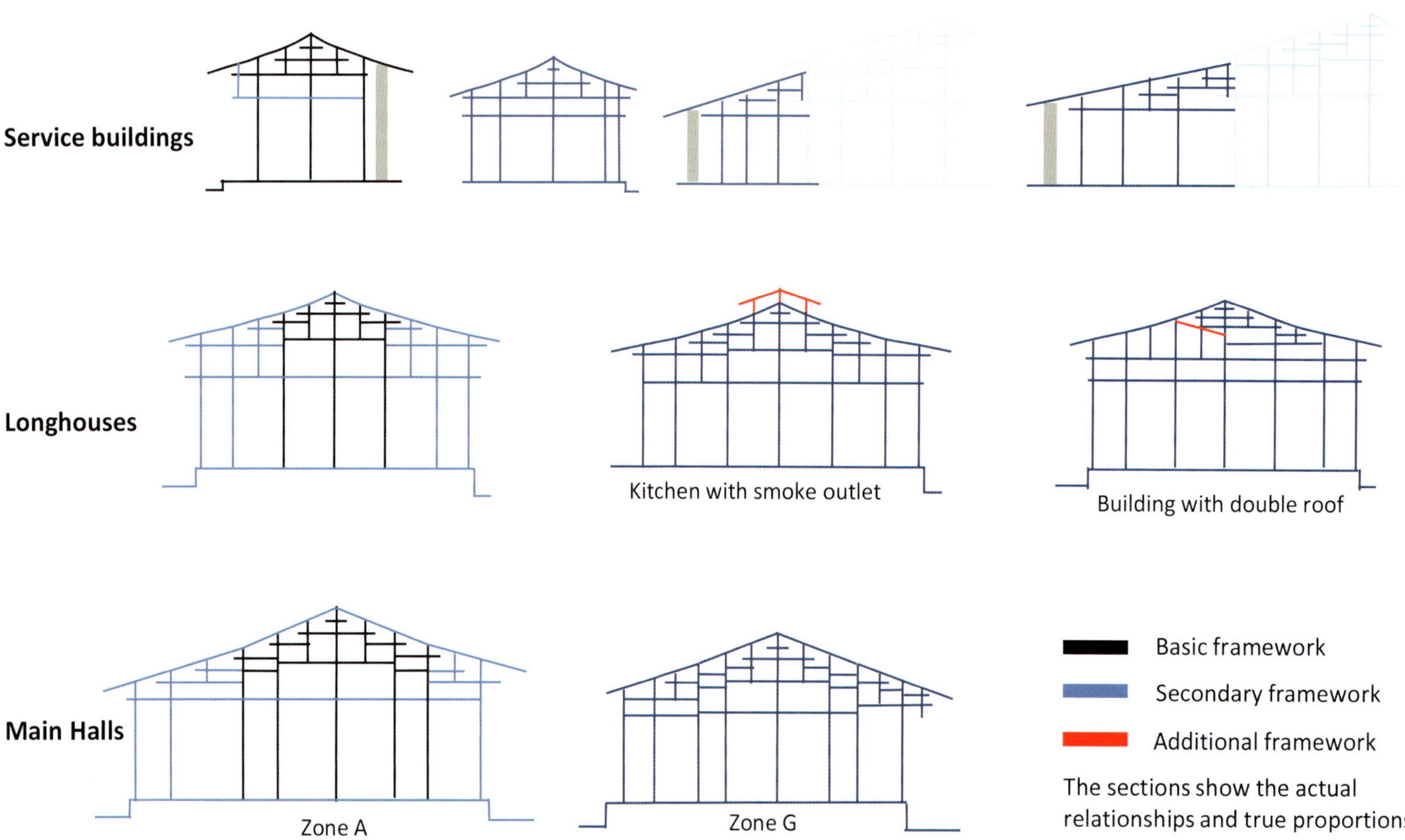

64. The site stepped down to several levels where buildings stand. There is a gap about 20 cm wide between the terrace's edge and Building 3's frame, which has been covered with a long bench.
65. The canals are arranged in N–S lines and parallel to each other. The terraces are not aligned E–W, but organised in an open »fan pattern«.
66. Buildings on two sides of a canal are not lined up.

Terraces and buildings

To mitigate dampness the buildings with raised timber floors were built over terraces. The bedrooms are raised between 0.3 m and 1 m from the ground. The setback distances between the edge of terraces and the line of buildings vary.

67. Longhouse B.
68–70. Raised wooden floors.

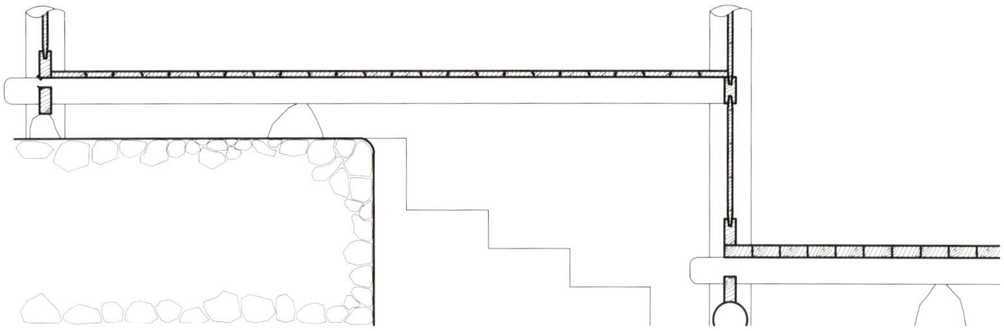

71. Longhouse E having the inside structure turned outwards.
72. Section through the central bay of the entrance hall, longhouse D.
73. Cross-section of longhouse E showing a »double-roof« and partial storey.
74. Double roof, Entrance Hall, longhouse B.

Hung ceiling as »double roof«

The entrance hall of longhouses has decorative elements. Under the roof of the entrance hall, a set of rafters is applied to create an appearance that the room has its own roof. The lower layer of the »double roof« is a ceiling – the overhead surface of the hall. The ceiling conceals the rough roof structure and adjusts the hall proportion. The double-roof design can be seen in longhouses of B, C, D and E.

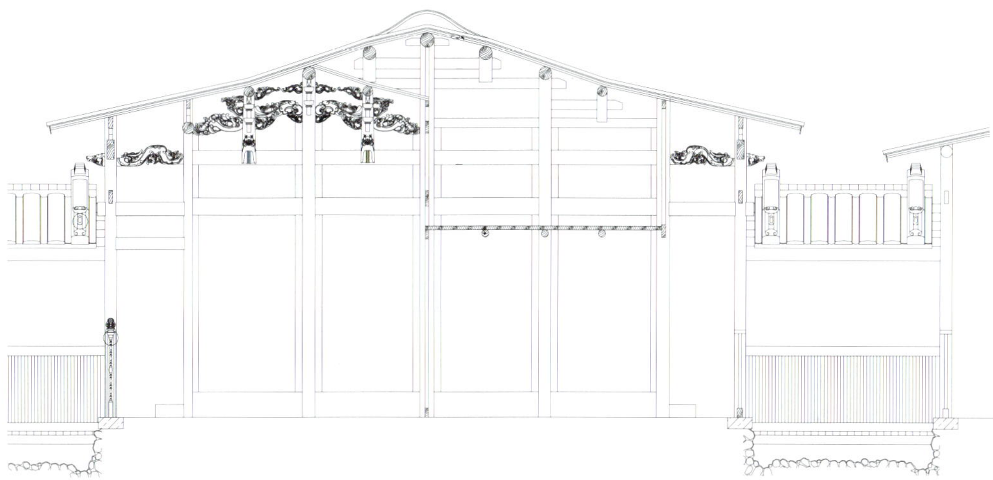

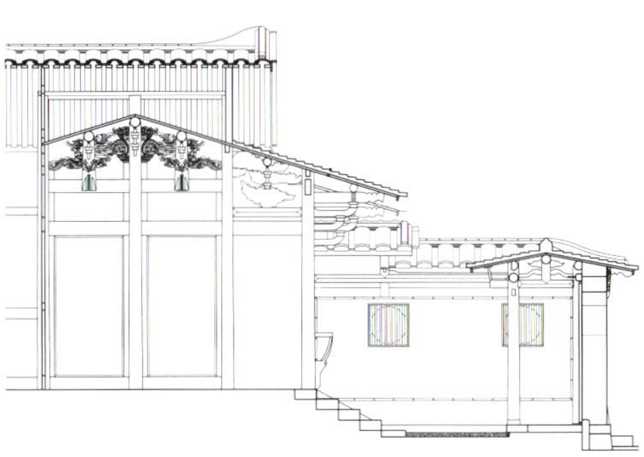

One and a half storey

Each longhouse has a loft space under its roof and above the ceiling, which is functioned as an airway for ventilation and as a mezzanine for safekeeping valuables.

The mezzanine is hiding behind the wall. Its floor joists are round logs stripped off their bark, protruding beyond the joints unevenly. This is a common practice: first, sections and lengths of structural members are only reduced when absolutely necessary; second, if a building is to be rebuilt, its timber members could be used in new applications.

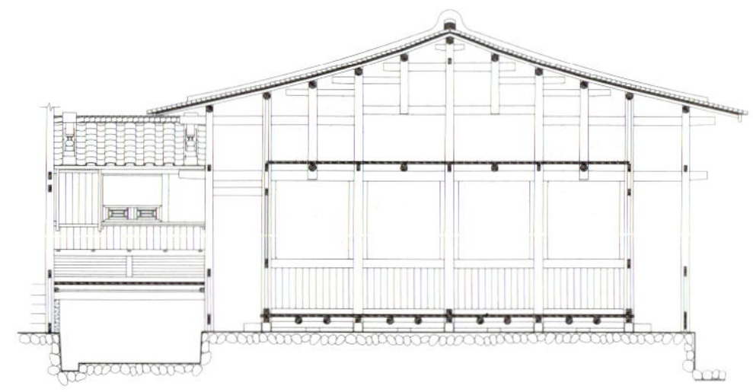

75. During the troubled times, this loft space was used for sleep.
76. The access to a mezzanine above an entrance hall is at the back by a ladder usually kept at a building corner. Longhouse H.
77. Untrimmed floor joists of mezzanine. Long side of longhouse D.
78. Section of longhouse B
79. Openings were made in the gable above the porch roof to allow light and air into the mezzanine, longhouse H.

78
75
76 77 79

80. Front view of longhouses of D and B.
81. Overhanging eaves supported by purlins, longhouse C.
82. Front view of the eave structure, longhouse B. The purlin of the lower eave spans from post to post, resting upon their projected brackets.

Roofed porch

A porch in a gable wall was constructed by adding eaves in three portions. The eaves are supported by their own posts to shelter an entrance and to complete the circulation around a building.

Eave structure

Eaves are the lower border of a sloping roof projecting beyond the post. It is interesting to look at the design closely. In the common area of the weiwu and that of the private quarters, brackets are used in the exterior part to support the deep eaves: four-tier and three-tier brackets extend over 1 m in the former and maximum 0.9 m in the latter. In longhouses, the overhanging eaves are supported by purlins laid on posts.

Additional eaves

An overhang eave runs across the width of a longhouse. Its weight is supported by pillars of the building, with or without additional posts.

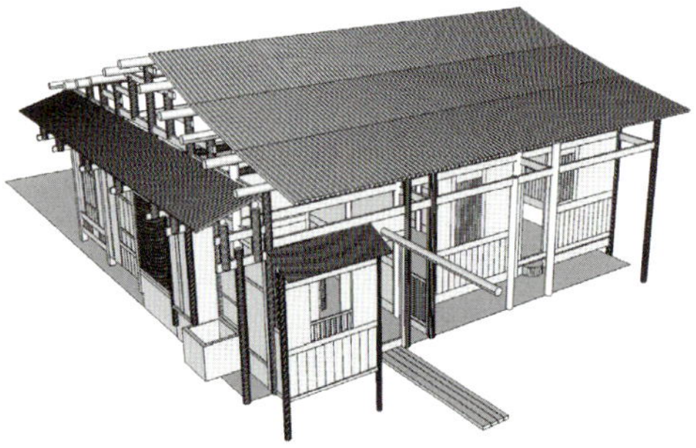

83. Rear eaves without additional posts, A bracket projected out from posts of the building to support eaves, balanced by a weight on the other side of the post. Longhouse D.
84. Additional eaves, longhouse F. One end of the long eaves extends more than the other end, the wider end has an additional post and the narrower end does not.
85. The eaves attached to the building is supported by additional posts, longhouse B.

86. Double window-I used in private units.
87, 88. Two examples of school windows.
89. Double window-II used in public spaces.
90. Mullioned window largely used to fill bridge walls.

87 88
86
89 90

Windows

All windows are wooden framed. Dafuzhen made no provision for papering over the frame. There appear to be two main types, mullion and lattice. The former is vertical members set in series, and the latter is a network of wooden strips.

The contrast between the aesthetic restraint of the longhouses and the ornate splendor of the common and school buildings could hardly be more pronounced in windows. Yet, both are impressive in their own ways, depending upon the circumstances.

There are several types used in the living quarters: (1) »double window-I« which is an opening filled with strips of wood and has a sliding blank panel installed inside to permit ventilation in summer and to give the occupants warmth in winter. (2) »double window-II« which is formed by two mullioned panels, both set on one track, can be slid one over the other to open or close the window. (3) mullioned window which is in-filled with diamond mullions.

Openings

The influence of »garden design« on the common areas is demonstrated by openings. A wooden frame made in the external wall of a public space admits light and air, as well as provides views from both sides.

91. View from zone A to longhouse C.
92–93.Windows of longhouse D, which can be opened, screened and closed. View from the courtyard towards East (left). The same windows view from outside (right).

Kitchen with a smoke vent

A longhouse houses several closely-related family units. They cook within their own kitchens. The oldest or original kitchen is the room at the rear of each longhouse, characterised by a smoke vent over roof. Firewood has been used for cooking with smoke rising from the cooking range. To let out the smoke, an opening is provided in the roof, which is sheltered by a small roof.

94. Kitchen is located on the upper terrace to give it access to fresh water running down from the hill. Longhouse D.
95. Kitchen, longhouse B.
96.Smoke produced by fire protects building against moisture and insects.
97. Tiled roof of a smoke vent, longhouse J.
98. Vent directs the smoke out through the top, longhouse D.

94
95 97
96 98

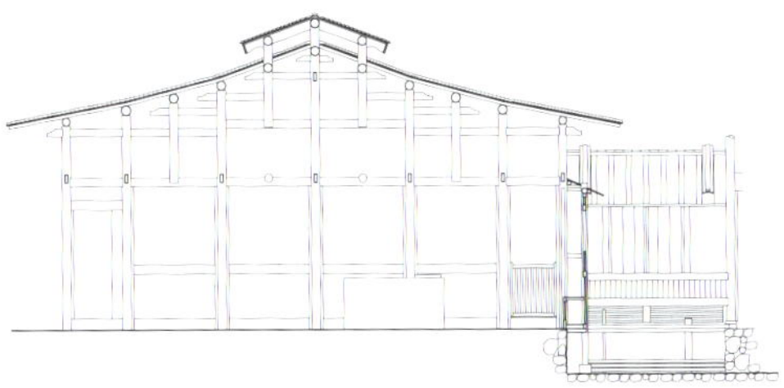

Cooking range

Cooking and eating are separated in terms of spatial arrangement. The kitchen is a woman's domain. The location of the cooking ranges has followed a number of different patterns: it could be parallel to kitchen walls, or positioned at an angle with respect to the wall, or by a wall, or at a corner. The reasons for this variation are not known for sure. Generally speaking, each has taken on its particular form and position for a variety of reasons, including the taste, demand and associations of some kind with which the cooking range became loaded.

99. Clay stove sets parallel to kitchen walls.
100. Stove positioned at an angle with respect to the wall.
101. Two stoves are perpendicular to each other: the big one is used for cooking an entire dinner and the small for warming breakfast in busy mornings.
102. L-shaped stove has three holes for pots at the top, fired by wood through two holes at the corner.
103. A new chimney was added to the stove, and clad in ceramic tiles.

104. Holes made for the basin, through which waste water flows from kitchen to a canal alongside the house.
105. The canal wall was built in two steps with pebbles.
106. Basin with two holes on the wall of a kitchen.

Basin and drain

In the kitchen there is no tap-water, but a masonry sink is used for rinsing vegetables and dish-washing. Built by the external wall, the sink is box-shaped and includes a drain to remove used water. A water supply system exists in the complex (see page 59).

Cabinets

A few cabinets have survived, built-in and moveable. The built-in cabinet is represented by a floor-standing or hanging kitchen cupboard consisting of shelves and a door used to keep dinnerware. The movable furniture is represented by bedroom wardrobes used together with chairs and tables.

107. Hanging case recessed / projected in the wall besides the opening for storage, bridge between C and E.
108. Cupboard built into the partition wall of a kitchen, which projects out from the wall, seen from the outdide., zone G.
109. Projected cabinet or altar, original function unknown. View SW flanking building from main hall, zone A.

110. B-B section showing the structures of longhouse I and privy.
111. Floor plan of longhouse I and privy.
112. C-C view.
113. A-A view.
114. View of longhouse I and the privy.
115. West wall of the privy.

Privy

At the northwest of the compound, a privy was built against lthe onghouse I's west wall. It is a minor timber structure, with a roof of single slope, dirt floor and wattle-and-daub walls.

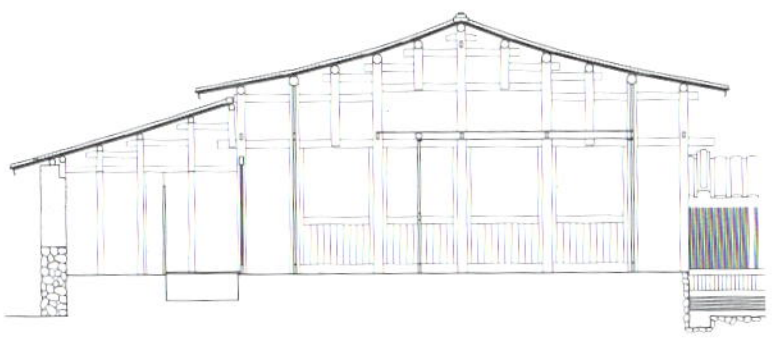

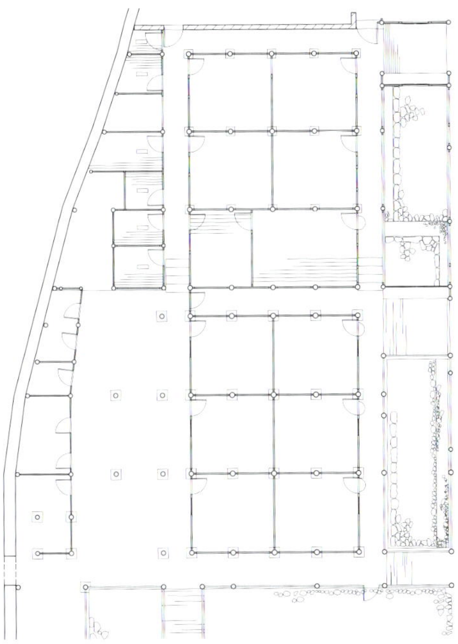

When entering a restroom, the user would put his or her belt over the door leaf to indicate that the space is occupied. Traditionally, cloth belts were common, made with different patterns for men and women.

Portable pots are used at night in bedrooms. The night pot for men is animal-shaped with a handle, usually shaped as a tiger, called tiger pot. The container for women is bowl-shaped with two handles. For the elderly, a chamber pot is built into a chair with a closable cover.

116. Additional privy outside the west exit.
117. In the privy building, there are a number of compartments which provide individual privacy.
118. Stone is used as stairs and post bases, untreated in the privy area. East privy.
119. Night pot, longhouse C
120, 121. Men's pot and woman's bowl (archaeological evidence).

116 119
117 118 120
121

122. A new concrete water tank was constructed within the compound wall, with water running through tubes for daily life.
123. The water storage has two openings in the stone wall, next to kitchens to allow easy access to the water.

Water management

Dafuzhen has a system of groundwater storage where walls were built at the bottom of geologic basins to hold back groundwater in the soil itself.

Drain canals

The canals carry away storm water. A drain c. 30 cm wide made for removing daily waste water and light rain also runs into the canal.

124. Examining the earthen terrace: 0.5–1.4 m high, the stone casing is c. 30 cm thick.
125. Pebbles are used for covering terrace walls and canal bottoms. They are laid diagonally to lock each other in place. The stone casing was carried out in sections. Each terrace corner was completed with bigger stones.
126. Open canals (2.9–2.2 m wide) entirely paved with smooth round pebbles taken from the Youxi brook. The canals are stepped and zigzagged, having a gentle slope to carry away water at certain flow rate and prevent washout after excessive rainfall.
127. Seepage well to hold storm water to prevent overflow is located near the lower end of zone A at both sides for torrential downpour.

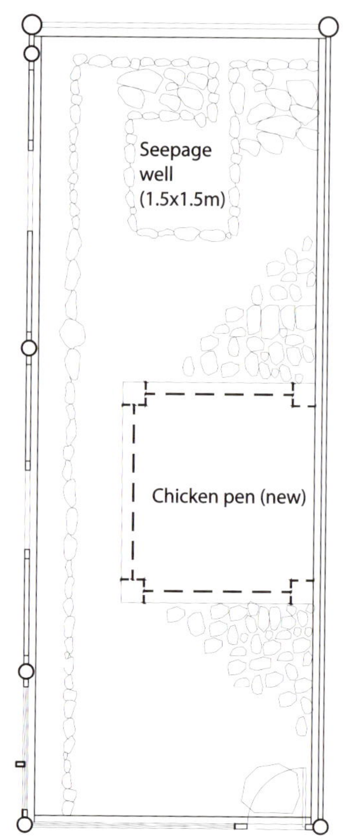

128. Small bathroom built over a canal, water discharges under its slatted floor into the canal.
129. In the rains, pigs were sheltering from the rain under the bridge.
130. Washing clothes in a standing basin.
131. Children taking a shower in the canal in hot summer.

Along the canal

Many standing basins are added by the canal. Washing and rinsing take place in the good drain area. Water is »piped« in from tanks.

The efficient weiwu residents raise small livestock in their homestead. The livestock space consists of a covered portion and a walled yard. In Dafuzhen, the canal is used as a »walled yard« – hens are kept at the higher part, and pigs at the lower. The bridge functions as a covered pig-sty.

Water outfall

Storm water is drained through canals to the farmland under gravity. The open space in front of zone A is paved where water is channelled through two underground discharge canals, parallel to each other.

132. The outfall of a covered channel, zone A (west side).
133. The end board of a floor above the canal can be removed for cleaning silt (inside the wall).
134. View the outfalls from outside (east side). The hole on the courtyard wall (right hand side) is for dogs.
135. Except zone A, water runs through an open ditch, zone G.
136. Section.

132		135
133	134	136

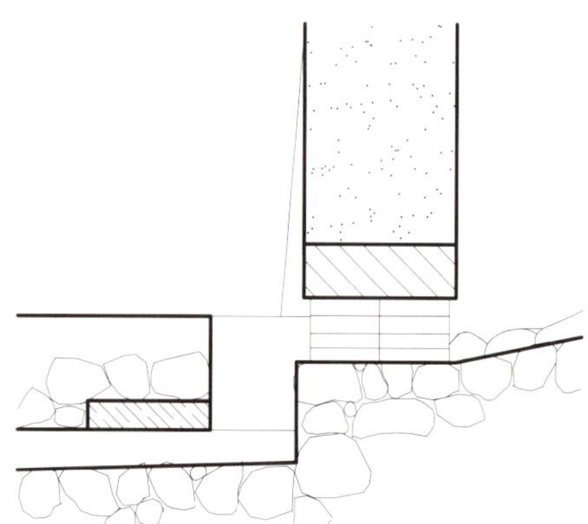

138. Bridges between longhouses. View at a cross bridge of the east canal.
137, 139. The bridge load is supported by long headstocks sitting on large stones which project beyond the masonry wall.

Roofed bridges

Bridges were built over canals to allow people to cross from one building to the other. Structurally, it is a pavilion with a roof, usually equipped with a bench, which also functioned as a meeting place where people could enjoy the cool air in summer.

The heights of buildings and terraces on two sides of a canal vary. For example, longhouse H: the heights of the eave-posts are 3.85 m (B1), 4.48 m (B2) and 4.16 m (B3) respectively; the heights of the terraces: 0.81 m (B1), 0.79 m (B2) and 0.68 m (B3). A prime function of the bridges to link the houses on each side at a suitable level.

140. Section of longhouse F and the east privy showing a bridge providing a passage between the two buildings of different sizes.
141. The south-most bridge between adjacent buildings (zone A and longhouse B). The eaves of B are higher than that of A.
142. Bridge between longhouses of B and D.
143. The bridge is a passage structure between two buildings. Steps are made between two levels.

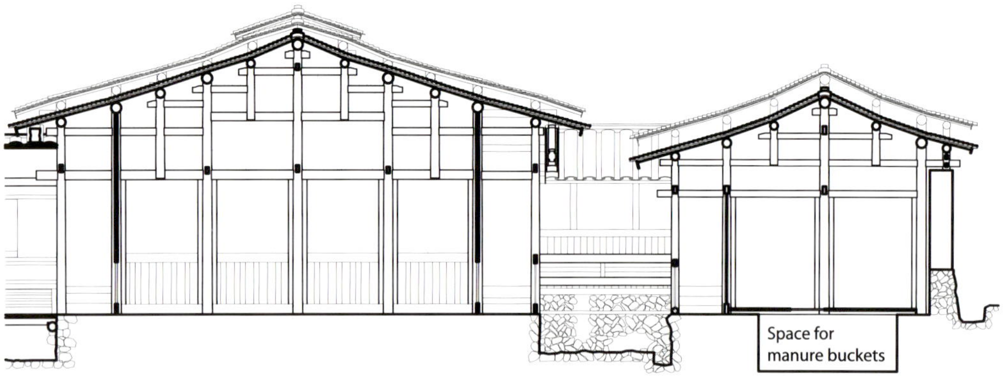

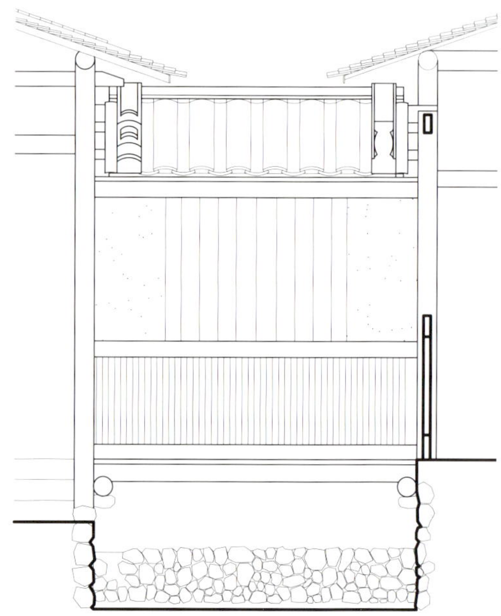

Types of the bridge structures

The roofed bridges may be broadly divided into two groups: 5-purlin and 7-purvilin according to their cross-sections. Our study reveals that each has a number of variations.

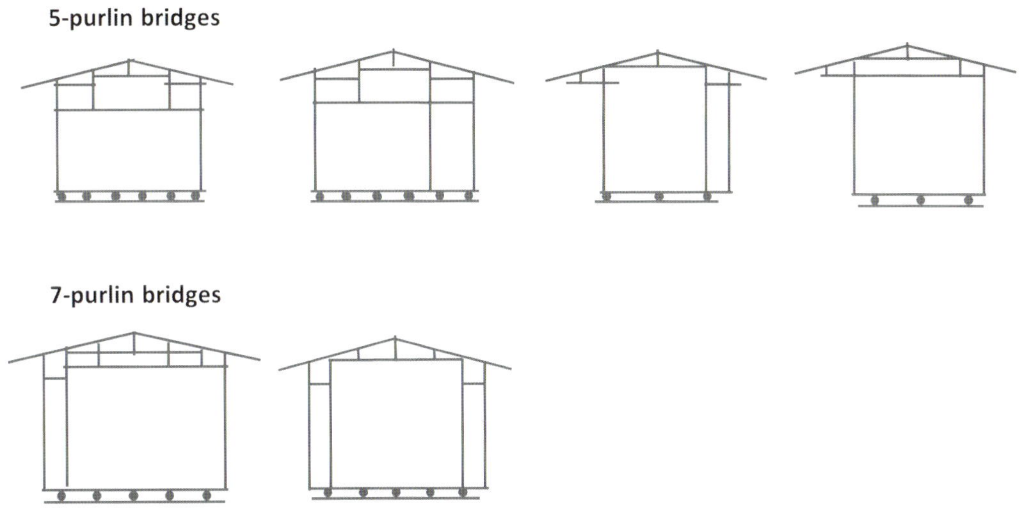

144. Schematic expressions of bridge types.

145. Several weiwu have been preserved in Youxi, one of them is Shujing built on a mountain. Viewed from the lower terrace over the canal to the upper bridge.

Roof structures

All bridges are roofed. The roof is supported by shared posts rather than its own. That is, its purlins are laid between the eave-beams of adjacent buildings to support the roof covering.

The roof structural design for each bridge is individual because structural details vary, even within a roof, since the adjacent buildings and terraces differ in height and do not line up in line.

146–148. Samples of bridge structures.

149. Many bridges became family space.
150. Bridge size: c. 3 m square, H: 2.5/3 m (eaves/ridge). One or two long benches are installed.
151. Bridge wall is filled with wooden slats to allow air circulation.
152. Double window of a bridge pavilion between zone A and longhouse C.

The bridges are passageways and shared spaces for social use of the residents. The bridge components, particularly the openings, are carefully designed and beautifully made. The bridge at the southeast side, of the longhouse C has a fan-shaped window opening to provide views of surrounding areas. This type of design was used in the old estate of the Xiao family too.

153. The fan-shaped window bridge between longhouses of C and E.
154. Picturesque view through the fan-shaped opening.
155. Landscape view from a bridge in the old estate.

156. Workshop and watchtower 2.
157. The subsidiary building's N-W corner towards watchtower 2 is cut off – a way of getting a complete view of the watchtower which is an iconic feature of Dafuzhen.
158. Marks left on the earthen wall are visible, which reveal that the wall was made by placing moistened earth into a frame and ramming it up layer by layer and one section next to the other. It is an ancient building method.
159. Section showing the timber structures and walls.
160. Floor plan, workshop.

156
157 159
158 160

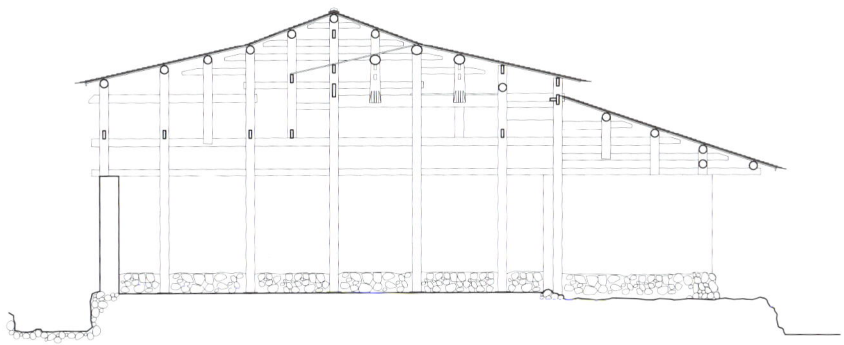

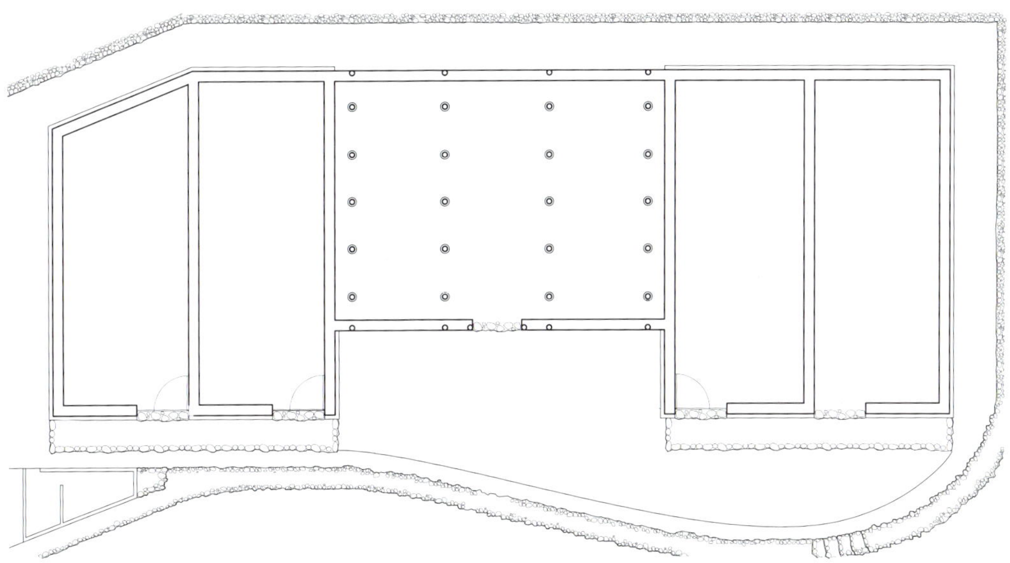

Workshop

Close to the weiwu on the east is a workshop with a total floor area of 326 sq. m. The workshop consists of three parts: a central building and two structurally independent subsidiary buildings in a symmetrical layout. Each subsidiary building has an lean-to which is a minor structure built against the front of the subsidiary building, with a roof of single slope.

The structure of the buildings is characterised by timber frameworks, tiled roofs and a dirt floor. The timber frame of the subsidiary buildings sits upon earthen walls, which were constructed on a stone base. Timber construction required considerable work on preparation of members, such as posts, beams, purlins and rafters, etc. The workshop was originally used to produce all wooden members before they were put together on site. The workshop was then used as a cattle house and barn.

Workmanship exercise

In the central bay of the building, a hung ceiling was made to create a pitched roof. The »double roof« practice was practiced in the workshop.

161–163. The ridge of the »double roof« with a *bagua* motif. The *bagua* is an emblem incorporating eight trigrams arranged octagonally around a symbol denoting the unification of yin and yang. The *bagua* was placed on the ridge for the luck of the family during the raising-ridge ceremony.

164. Roof framing, main hall, zone A.
165. Measured drawing showing the sections of the ridge and purlins, main hall, zone A.
166. Block and bracket support a purlin, zone A.

164 165
166

Entasis profiled ridge-beam

In the central bay of the buildings located on the central axis, the ridge and purlins are entasis – wide in the middle and narrow at each end. The main ridge is bigger than the purlins in diameter. The end of the ridge and purlins is supported by blocks and brackets. All these features can also be seen in the old estate.

Aspects that are less clear are first, the compound is not orientated true N–S; second, several buildings had their corners cut out. While there must be reasons for these phenomena, they do not necessarily have functional explanations, but may be explained by the Fengshui theory.

According to the Fengshui theory, people's fate was determined by the date and time of one's birth. There are two major categories: the east-four fate and the west-four fate according to the locations of the fate stars, corresponding eight orientation patterns. Each pattern consists of eight directions to describe the positions of the lucky and unlucky stars.

Dafuzhen fits one of the eight orientation patterns. In the diagram shown here, lucky orientations are in white and unlucky in shade. The lucky directions are suitable for entranceways, so that luck will come in. No door openings should be made in unlucky areas. The cut-out corners must be arranged with due regard for effects of fortune.

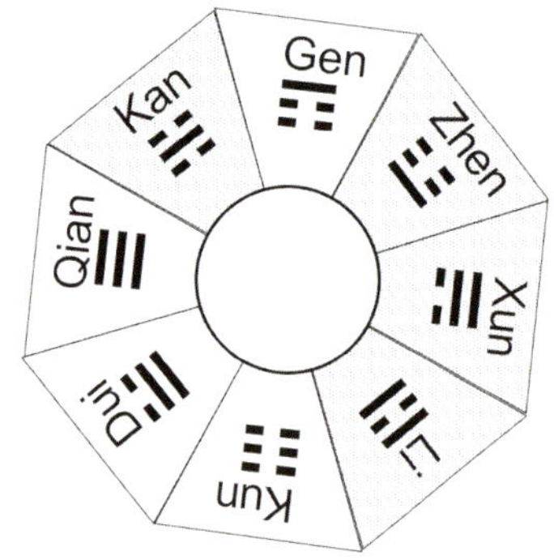

Lucky, suitable location for entrance

Unlucky, privy, kitchen

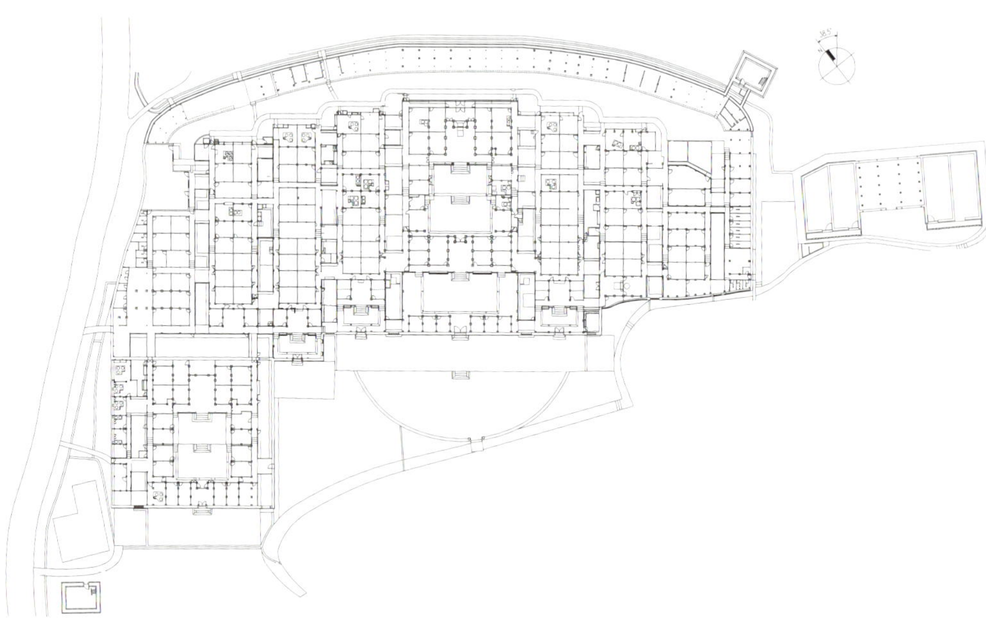

167–172. Building-corners cut off.
169. Fu-de position.

173. Ditch around the wall, looking east.
174. Roof of the east privy and storage.
175. Plan of the north wall and the shed.
176. North wall, looking west.
177. Section of the covered storage and privy arranged along the wall.
178. Elevation of the buildings inside the east wall.

169
167 170
171
168 172

175
176
173 177
174 178

Enclosing earthen walls

The weiwu is enclosed by a rammed-earth wall built upon a stone base. Along the wall a shed was constructed. The shed roof shelters the earthen wall. The covered area is earthen floored used for various purposes.

The earthen wall does not bear the load of the roof but its own weight. The wall was constructed by a stone base at the lower part and rammed earth wall above (30–40 cm thick). A ditch is excavated around the wall to receive water dropped from the eaves and to carry it away.

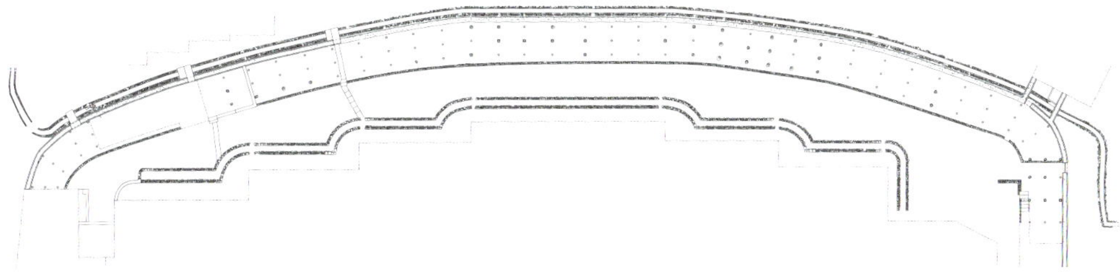

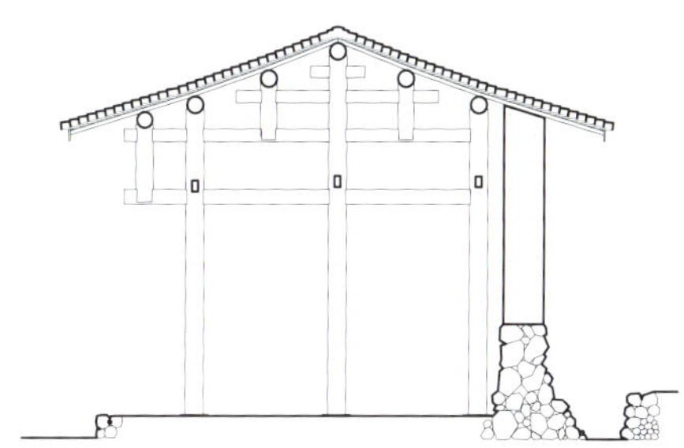

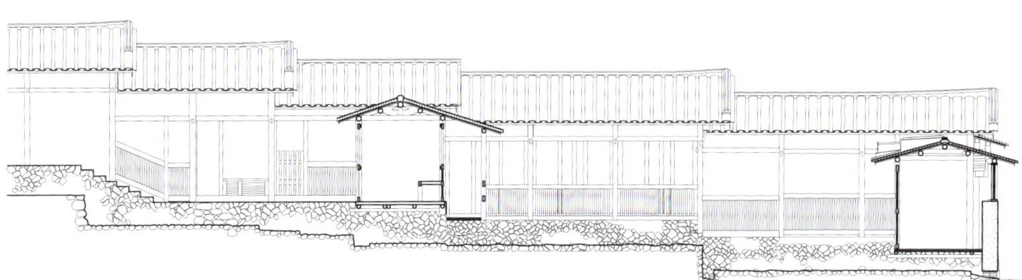

Covered storage

The shed building positioned along the central axis consists of seven bays, and is taller than the others located on both sides. Its central bay is 3.4 x 2.8 m in plan and rest bays are 2.8 x 2.8 m; H: 2.7/3.6 m (eaves/wooden ridge). Blocks and brackets are used to hold the front eaves-purlin. Two roofs of different heights meet with an angle, and they share a transverse frame at the junction.

In this place harvested crops were stored, which is now a cluttered space.

179. Transverse frame at the junction of two roofs.
180. Covered storage, looking east.
181. Central-bay eaves.

182. Ramming poles and distributing carriers.
183. The side and rear walls without coating showing layers of construction.

Wall construction

In the wall construction of the compound, the workshop and the watchtowers, the basic building materials are earth and stone. The procedure for wall building was as follows: The moist earth was put into a moulded space, pushed into all the corners and compacted with a wooden pole with a rammer head on one end and a spear head on the other. The mould was raised up when one layer of compaction was finished. The wall is about a half meter thick at the base, but tapering towards the top.

Watchtowers

The estate is enclosed by earthen walls and fortified with watchtowers. Thre were originally three, now two watchtowers remain.

184. Tower 2, looking north.
185. Watchtower 2 at far left, looking southeast.
186. Section of Tower 2.

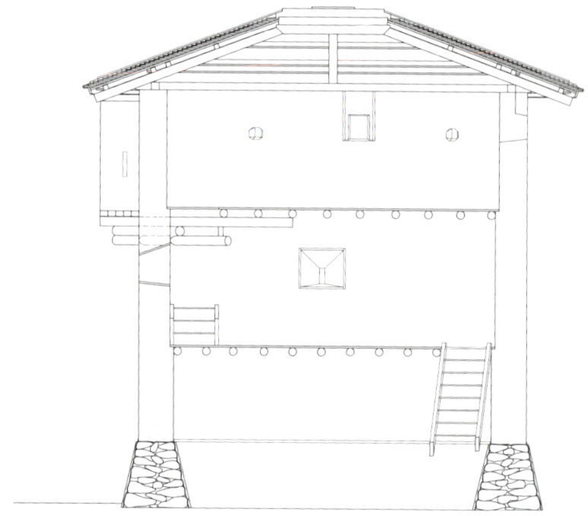

187–189. Tower 1. Roof: Pyramidal roof, size: 6.8 x 5.2 m (plan); wall thickness: 0.56 m (ground level); H: 6.9 m (ground to eaves).

The main defence was provided by watchtowers: two at the rear of the enclosure, outside the corners (one missing), and one in front of the school. The watchtower is a freestanding structure consisting of three levels, with interior staircases. The thick earthen wall has a shoulder to receive floor boards. On the top level, there are two small mud-brick structures jutting out the opposite corners of the tower, where the guards could keep a watch for approaching attackers. Openings were made in the walls to allow them to shoot to defend the estate. The earthen walls are fire-proof and strong, but susceptible to water damage. They therefore require regular maintenance.

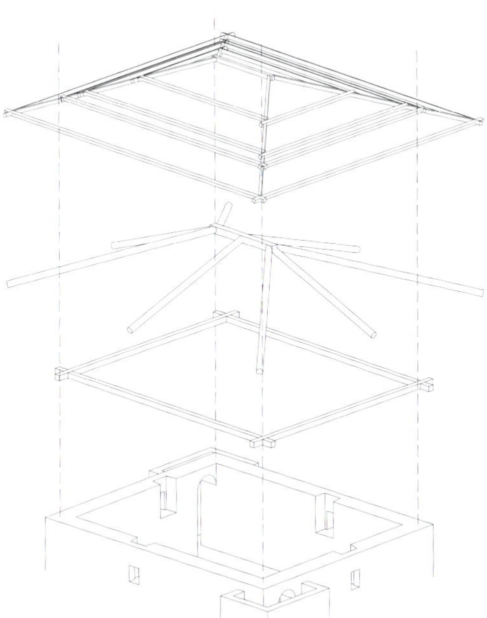

A small overhanging structure at a corner of the watchtower, with lookout holes, affords watching both sides but is difficult to see into from outside.

There are gun-slits, thin vertical openings, in walls of the tower. The wall behind the opening is cut away at an oblique angle, so that the defender has a wide field of view and can shoot in all directions.

190–195. Tower 2. Roof: hip roof; size: 6.4 x 5.3 m (plan); wall thickness: 0.58 m (ground level); H: 6.7 m (eaves).

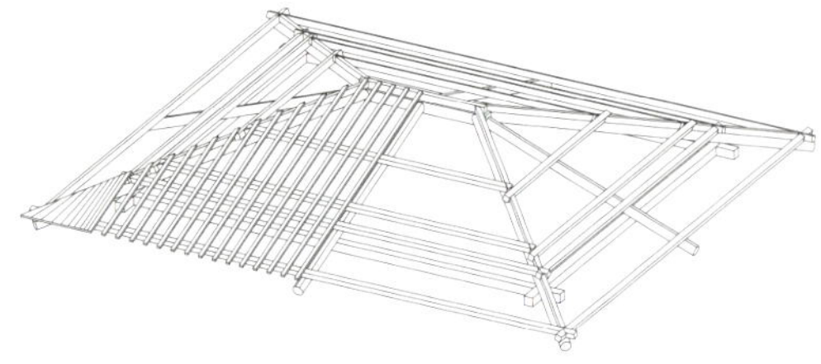

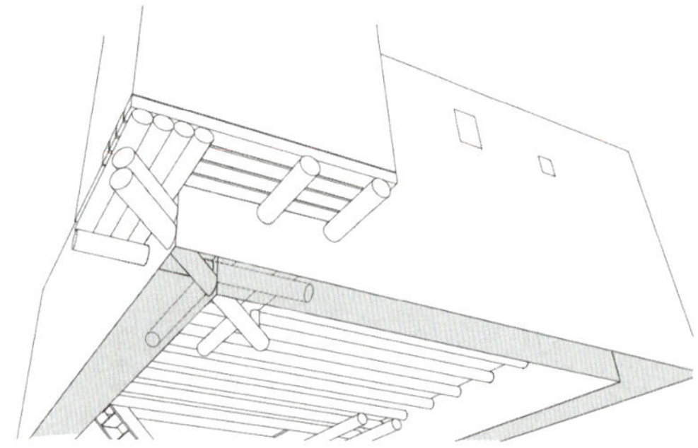

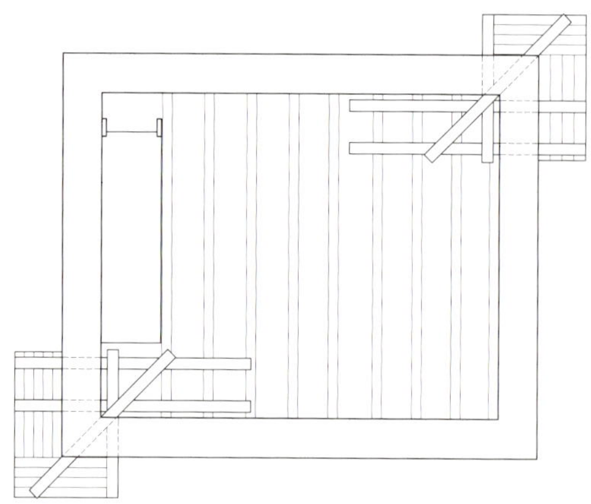

Unseen details

Beams: visible and concealed faces

The central bay of a building is a formal living room where beams are elaborately carved against the plaster wall, and block-brackets are used on the underside of the ridge and purlines. However, the reverse side of the beams seen on the other side of the wall is not treated. Usually they are not load bearers.

1. Decorated beams, Entrance Hall, longhouse B.
2. View from side bay towards the central bay of the main hall, zone A.

3. In roofing of service buildings – workshop, storage and privy, rafters (10 x 2 cm in section) are placed c. 10 cm apart.
4. In eaves construction, rafters are laid without any space in between, for the principle elevation of the complex.
5. Smoke-blackened kitchen where bricks are placed upon rafters, upon which tiles are laid.
6. Rafters are closely spaced upon purlins, with battens covering the gaps over the edges of the parallel rafters, main hall, zone G.

3 5
4 6

»Overbuilt« and »underbuilt« roof

A roof consists of three components: purlins, rafters and tiles. Positioned on the purlins, the rafters run from the ridge to eaves, onto which roof tiles are laid. The sloping roof surface is straight rather than curved. The way of rafter placement in main buildings is »overbuilt« – higher than average, whereas in service buildings it is »underbuilt« – lower than normal.

Tiled roofs

In Fujian, driving rains are frequent. Tiled roofs are constructed to protect timber-framed buildings; eaves are projected to help protect floor and doors. Dafuzhen buildings, big and small, are all covered with tiles. The roofs are all pitched, many with lean-to at gable ends.

7. Viewed from above, longhouses of D, longouse B, and zone A.
8. Roof plan.

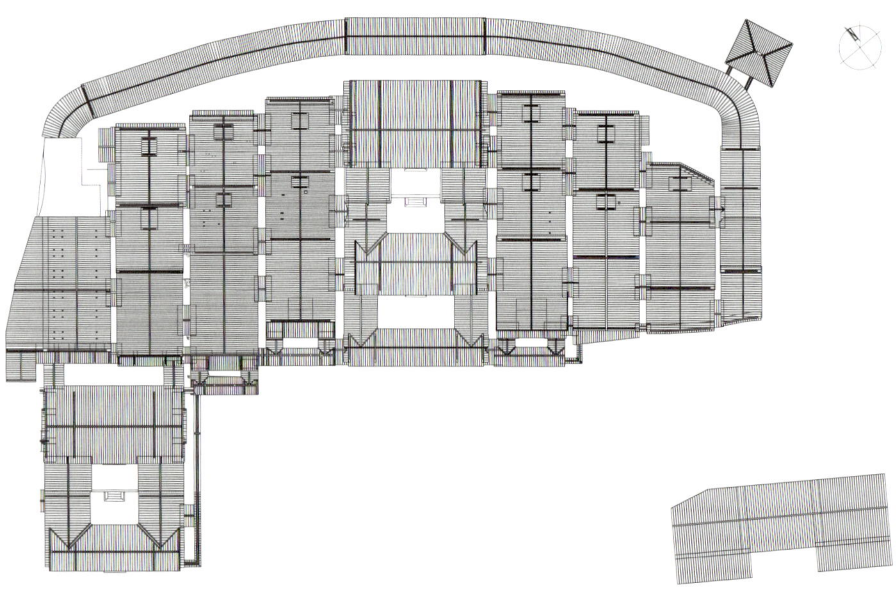

9. Curved ridge. The curves were designed geometrically by formulae regarded as tiler's mastery. Entrance Hall, zone G.
10. The main ridge is entirely plastered and painted which is characterised by a blue colour scheme. Main hall, zone A.
11. Ridge of flanking building is elaborated creating a complex pattern which was probably derived from »tracing clouds floating in the atmosphere«, zone G.

Tiled ridges

Ridges were made of tiles varying in design and details. The ridge of the main hall has a plastered surface which is colourfully painted; whereas that of the flanking building is »carved«, and that of the storage is rough, being deliberately fine and rustic respectively.

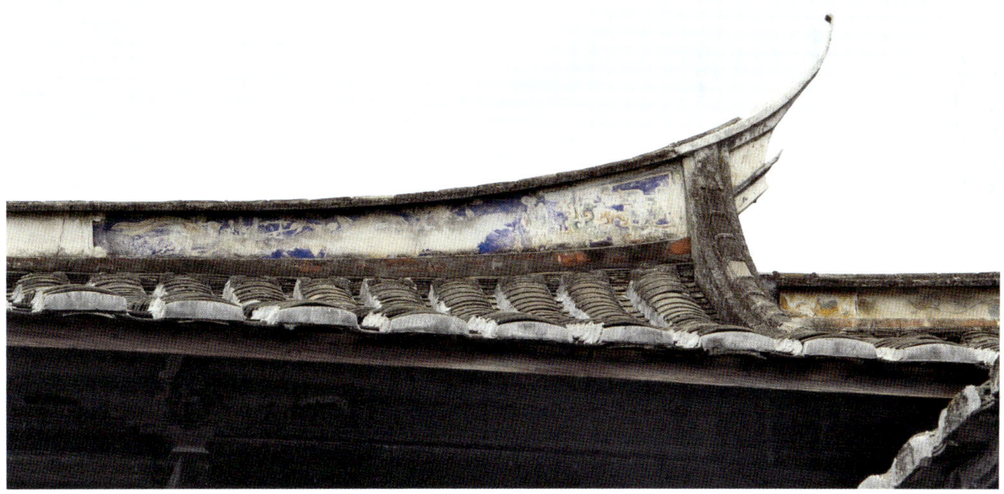

12. Two pitched roofs intersect at S-E corner of longhouse C.
13. A trough along gable, kitchen, longhouse F.
14, 15. Ridges of the entrance hall and the flanking building intersect, and the roofs form a valley on each side of the ridge. The two ridges differ in design. Under the pitch roof at the gable end there is a zigzag ridge (see right). S-W corner, zone G.

12 13
14 15

16. **Method 1** used in private foreyards: under tiles laid in a row on a valley rafter to form a valley. Foreyard of longhouse B.
17. **Method 1.** Underside of eaves: Eaves tiles overhang over the valley rafter. Foreyard of longhouse B.
18. **Method 2** used in common courtyards: A valley wherein under and cover tiles sit in three rows.
19. **Method 2.** The valley rafter is supported by brackets projected in tiers that are perpendicular to each other. Zone A.

16 17
18 19

Valleys

A valley is formed by the intersection of two inclined sides of a roof. The valleys of the courtyard architecture were made in two ways applied to the common courtyards and the brothers' respectively.

Parapets

A parapet is a low guarding wall along the edge of a gable roof to block rain water. It is often plastered and painted. Parapets can be grouped by position:

Group 1: Parapet of a flanking building under the eaves of a main hall.
Group 2: Parapet between adjacent flanking buildings built on different terraces.
Group 3: Parapets employed in foreyards of longhouses.
Group 4: Parapets used on bridges.

There is a coherent roof drainage system, viewed from this standpoint; the tiled roofs, valleys and parapets are designed to collect water and remove that water.

20. **Group 1**: On a slopied roof, the upper part of a parapet is triangle shaped to fill up the gap; under the eaves of a main hall, the lower part is decorated.
21, 22. Side and frontal view of a parapet, zone A.

23. **Group 2**: The parapet is parallel to the gables of flanking buildings, zone A.
24. Detail of figure 23: the lower part of the parapet.

Group 3: Parapets are employed in foreyards of longhouses to make the space ambience. The longhouse entry is associated with receiving guests, the parapet adds a simple ornamental touch to the domestic interior. They were made of tile and plaster in the shape of stylised plants or animals. They therefore could be called according to their distinctive parapets: »banana leaf«, »herbivorous dragon« and »sea fish«.

25. Sea-fish yard, the foreyard of longhouse D enclosed by structures of different height. The sea-fish parapet is under the eaves of the entrance hall.

26. Banana leaf shaped parapet. Longhouse C.

27. Herbivorous dragon which hung round the building as protection with its power. Longhouse B.

28. Symmetrical silhouette of a bridge.
29. Parapet detail.
30. A parapet comprises of three sections; its thickness is gradually decreased towards eaves to reduce the dead load.
31. There is a parapet at either end of the roof. The two are not the same in shape.

Group 4: Parapets of a roofed bridge built between longhouses, that are all similar but not identical.

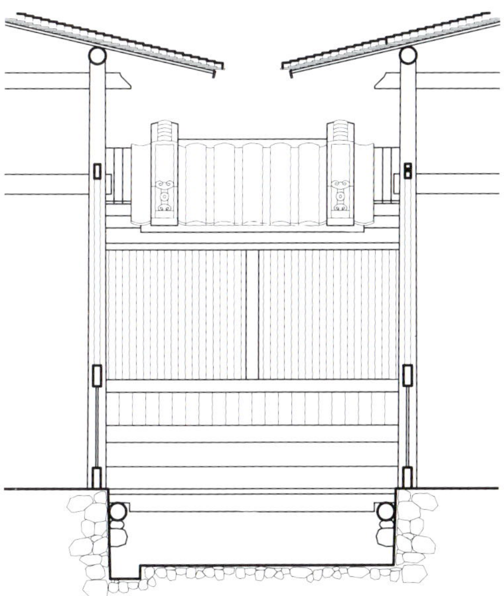

Rear views of parapets

The parapet was made of tiles. Its exterior face is usually covered by a layer of plaster; the other face is exposed.

32. Parapets were originally unplastered (Shujing).
33. Partially covered parapet, bridge next to Kitchen D.
34. Rear view of a bridge parapet.

35. The parapet of a roofed bridge nearly touches a beam of longhouse E. The fact suggests that the parapet was not original, but added after the building and the bridge were completed.
36. Between longhouses of H and I and zone G, there are two bridges. The ridges of the bridges are awkwardly bumping against the eaves of the longhouse, which suggests that they were later added.
37. Close-up view of a parapet of a flanking building attached to the main hall, zone A, which bears witness to the change – the parapet was a later addition.

Modifications or additions

Many details reveal that the compound had undergone modifications or additions. Over the years, the weiwu has had additions. As we know that the construction work lasted for about 10 years, the estate was built or added in stages.

Tiles, bricks and their applications

Tiles and bricks are grey in colour. The tiles are slightly curved used as both under- and cover-tiles. Roof ridges are protected by coping bricks, double-beveled to shed water. Rectangular bricks are used to build masonry structures.

38. Coping bricks used as the top course on a main ridge / gable ridge.
39. Canal wall is a masonry structure. Bricks are used to form the lower half of the wall, laid in a in different pattern for ventilation.
40. Tiles are alternatively used as under tiles and cover tiles.
41. Roof tile. There is only one type, 23 x 22 x 1 cm.
42. Double-beveled coping having a two-sloped top surface with its high point along the centre ridge. Size: 22 x 10 x 5 cm.
43. Brick, 23 x 11 x 3 cm.

38 39
40 41
42
43

44. Edges of the tiles were moulded with mortar. Longhouse E.
45. Four windows with vertical bars in the gable wall of longhouse C. Tiles are vertically placed as a facing to cover the joint between the gable wall and gable eaves. The facing tiles are finished with plaster mouldings.
46. Tiles are placed over a junction of a roof and wall to cover the gap, longhouse D.

Facing tiling

Tiles are used to cover roofs, walls, and the junction between them, to protect them from rainwater penetration.

Gutters

Walking into Dafuzhen in January 2012, we found many interesting details, such as members attached to eaves, but did not know what and why, so decided to closely examine them.

The wooden members under eaves we noticed and puzzled about in 2012 that turned out to be gutter supporters. A gutter of wood or bamboo set immediately below and along the eaves to catch and to carry away the rainwater from the roof. Many of the gutters have already disappeared. The guttet supports have survived their gutters.

47. Wooden gutter, front view.
48. Bamboo gutter, bird's-eye view.
49, 50. Bamboo gutter with a hole which might be connected to a downpipe to divert rainwater.

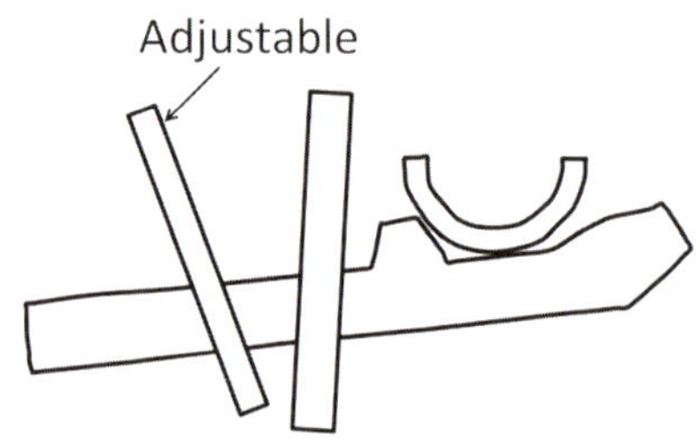

51. Water tank near the kitchen of longhouse B.
52. Tank next to longhouse F for storing water.
53. A bamboo gutter which might be connected to a downpipe (now missing) to conduct water to a tank.

Water tanks

Tanks were built at the higher part of the settlement to store rainwater collected from roofs, or stream water fed by canals in wet seasons. The water management enabled natural water supply and drainage, as well as irrigation.

Skylight

The skylight is an opening made on the roof to let in light. Two types of skylights can be seen in Dafuzhen. One is fixed, sheltered by a canopy formed by tiles. Another is moveable, glazed by a piece of glass.

54. Openings protected by rain caps. Main hall, zone A.
55. A rain cap is formed by tiles cantilevered in a corbelling manner (Shujing).
56. A triangular frame, moveable and glazed to allow light, longhouse C.

57, 58. Kitchen high windows, basketwork functioned as a fly-screen mesh, longhouse B.
59. Window frame with bamboo strips woven around vertical bars. Kitchen, longhouse G.

High windows

Kitchen openings are installed high above the floor to admit natural light and draught. A typical type is bamboo slatted windows, which is a frame with vertical bars woven around by bamboo strips.

Bamboo-work

Bamboo is one of main materials used in the region. The products were all homemade including furniture, homeware and dishware. They are beautiful and durable. Many old techniques have declined in the rapidly industrialising country. However, the bamboo-work tradition is still alive.

Walls: bamboo-daub infill

Bamboo is a substantial material for building, particularly, bamboo infill wall. The wall is not load-bearing. Bamboo panels fill the spaces within the wooden frame. The iprefabricated infill is a woven lattice of bamboo strips. A mixture of mud, sand and straw is then applied to the surfaces onto both sides.

Bamboo pegs

Bamboo pegs are used to fix a member in place. For example, a board hangs from the projecting end of a gable roof, which is fixed with bamboo pegs, usually a group of five, to purlins

60. Bamboo strips wrapped with ropes are fixed to the post-and-beam frame as bases for mud plastering.
61. Materials used are timber post, stone base, wooden frame, bamboo panel and mud plaster.
62. Gable board used to protect purlins, which is secured with bamboo pegs.
63. Handmade bamboo pegs, Kaiyuansi, Quanzhou.

64. A door knocker of the main entrance, zone A.
65. Front door of longhouse D (seen from inside).

Entrance doors

The door is constructed of vertical planks which are joined together by treenails shaped like a dove's tail. The wooden door has a pair of vertical pins protruded at the top and bottom of the leaf. The pins are fitted into stone sockets to hold its position. A bar is fixed inside on each door leaf to lock it; a door knocker is fixed outside.

A pair of door-gods are painted on the door, and a paper strip of talisman significance attached to it, to keep evils away.

Room doors

Three types of doors have been distinguished: solid door, divided door and half door. The divided door and the half door are used in longhouses and flanking buildings. The divided door consists of two separated leaves, one over the other. The leaves may be operated independently. The half door is used to restrict children to move out through it.

Door fixings

The doors are fixed in place in two ways: hinge and pivot. The former was made of metal and the latter wood.

66–68. A solid door is constructed of vertical boards fastened by a frame. It can be locked from both sides. Flanking buildings.
69. Door connected to its frame by a hinge which consists of two rings jointed together by a pin. Side-door, zone A.
70. Pivot bearer made of wood with carving. Rear door at main hall, zone A.

66 67 68
69 70

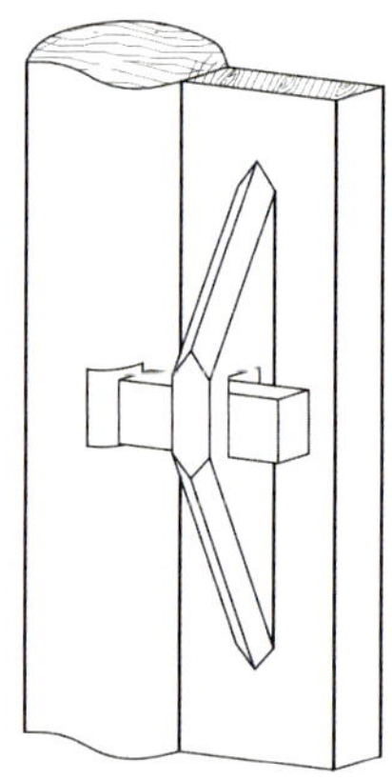

71, 72. Stone filters or drain covers, carved in pattern, fit on drainage pipes.
73. In courtyard, a gentle slope directs rainwater to a covered drain, usually at corner.
74. A shallow groove at the end of the upper terrace to channel water flowing down.

Drainage system

Canals, open or covered, above or below ground, straight, curved or zigzagged are employed in Dafuzhen for drainage purposes.

Underground channels

In courtyard architecture, drain pipes were buried in platforms of main buildings to remove rainwater from a courtyard through the building to a given area.

75, 76. A channel buried in the platform of the mid-hall (left); the outfall after rain (right), zone A.
77, 78. Outfall on the external wall of zone G.

79. Circular hole in the middle of a room, where there is a junction of underground channels. Entrance building, zone G.

Maintenance holes

The underground channel has a maintenance hole, built indoor with a cover, which is an access point for performing maintenance and/or inspection on pipes buried below ground.

Building materials

The design of Dafuzhen is made more complex by a diversity of materials. The materials employed in its construction are timber, earth, bamboo, stone, cobbles and tiles.

The local tree species for structures are fir and pine (post dia. 18/16/14 cm). Earth is used for perimeter walling. Stone is used along platform edges, and as stairs and post bases; cobbles used for covering terraces and canals. Bamboo is used for partitions, and tiles are used for roofing.

Stonework

Stones are used as foot blocks of posts, and used in platform construction, as well as canal wall building.

80. Masonry work used in flanking buildings are: cylinder-shaped post bases, semi-circled step stones and stone slabs enveloped the platform, zone A.
81. Squared stones were used to build the lower part of a canal wall in a diamond pattern above brick outlets.
82. Stone base, main hall, zone A. High-quality stonework is characteristic of buildings in the common area.
83. Upper part of a canal wall filled with stone lattice finely shaped as bamboo for ventilation.

80 82
81 83

84. Struts overhanging from the projecting roof frame are terminated by carved lotus, Entrance Hall, zone G.
85. Double tie-beams are used between posts to support the eaves. The upper one is shaped as a fish dragon – dragon head and fish body, Entrance Hall, zone G.
86. Beam end shaped in profile resembles a phoenix's head, First courtyard, zone A.
87. There is an entire railing system along the edges of the canal. The baluster of the handrail outside the open bay of longhouse E is enriched with carved lotus.

84 86
85 87

Wooden ornament

Architectural ornaments are employed in common zones to enhance the important effect of the main halls. Three groups of details have been selected as superior examples: roof-frame members, timber partitions and wooden furniture. The wood carvings are of vegetation motif and zoomorphic theme. They serve as symbols for protection.

88. An offering table with stylised decoration in the entrance hall. Furniture making was popular in the country in the Ming-Qing time. The design appears to have been intended to accommodate current decorations, longhouses C.
89, 90. Veranda along the south side of the main hall has a railing which is partly decoration and partly divider. The rail structure consists of panels and their sustaining studs and are highly ornamental. Zone A.
91, 92. Carving requires skilled craftsmanship. Photos taken at Ye Benying's workshop in Quanzhou, Fujian, 2014. A beam under fabrication, which is engraved with a pattern of dragons.

Postscript

Throughout our survey, we have seen how Dafuzhen responded to the challenges of terrain and water, and what architectural vocabulary was adapted to ensure family unity and harmony. In Dafuzhen, the private longhouses are closely packed together, woven by a network of verandas, corridors and bridges, and connecting to the central-positioned and well-proportioned public buildings and courtyards.

Dafuzhen was urban in character, following planning traditions found in cities. The basic structures, that is the longhouse and cannel as units, have ramifications for the ordered layout. The dense settlement is separated from the surrounding farmlands by massive walls, so that not a bit of the rich land is »wasted«. Dafuzhen was designed to utilise the water given by Mother Nature, so that no water is »wasted«.

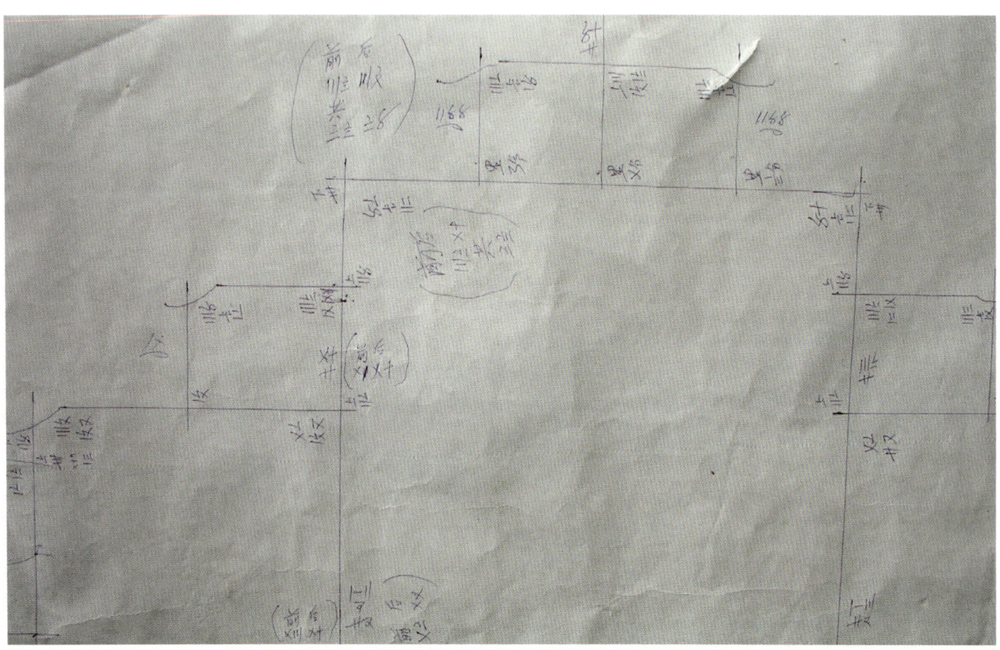

1, 2. Working drawing on paper which shows a transverse framework; all information is given in numerical symbols and professional codes. The framework design is vital, to which floor plan is inextricably linked. Fu'an, Fujian.

3, 4. Carpenters' symbols written with a bamboo pen; carpenter's tools: plane, ink marker, bamboo pen and L-ruler, Quanzhou, Fujian.

Is vernacular architecture »an architecture without architects«? Dafuzhen was designed and built by local artisans. The design drawings of Dafuzhen did not survive. But, working drawings and carpenter's poles (or ruler) have long been known as common practice among the professionals. Their design skills, fine craftsmanship and special solutions to local building problems are passed from one generation to another.

Specialized guilds persist in Fujian, each with its own master. A number of traditions can still be seen today, distinguished from each other in design methods and drawing techniques. Specialist knowledge is protected and available only to the in-group of workmen.

Module

A modular is a standard unit used in planning, design and fabrication. The courtyard architecture has a modular system within which a courtyard is an allied module. The private buildings were built using 3-bay bilding as a unit. The unit can be detached, or joined to form one building according to desire or topography. The interior space is partitioned with nonloadbearing walls or ceilings. The modular unit (or 3-bay building) can be increased or reduced by adding or removing one or two bays. This is done without altering the design. In reality modular construction is a viable method of prefabrication. The final actual dimensions are all recorded on a long, thin piece of wood called *gaochi*.

Gaochi

Gaochi is a carpenter's ruler, designed and used by a master carpenter. It is usually 3–4 m long, 9–12 cm by 2–4 cm in cross-section, made of fir. It contains lines, marks or symbols to measure dimensions of structural members in 1:1 scale. The master carpenter marks all measurements on the ruler. The architecture, drawing and the *gaochi* together are architectural heritage as an entity. From our architectural viewpoint, the weiwu is not only essential to acknowledge, but also preserves high quality of design and planning, with technical and aesthetic sophistication.

5–9. Two *gaochi* are kept under the eaves at Shujing. Numerical symbols and professional marks are stated on the rulers.

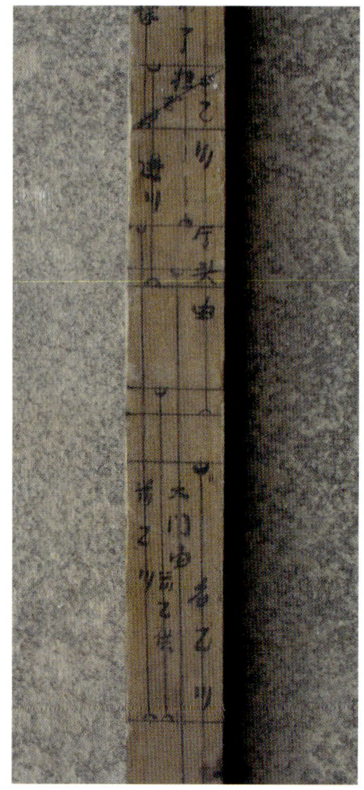

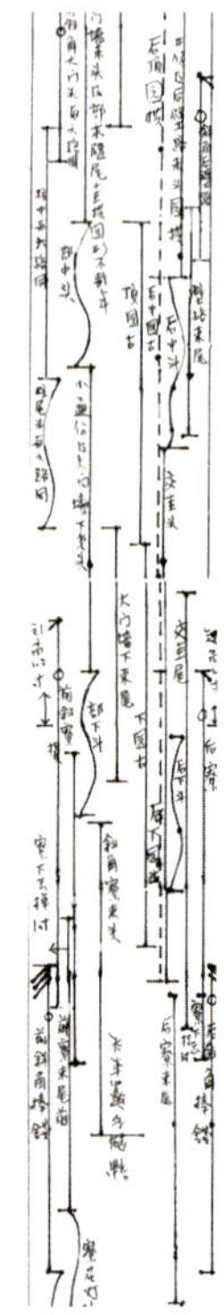

10–12. Frames were assembled on the ground and then raised by communal effort, and lashed securely, one by one. All building members and component parts were made prior to assembly. Shunji community temple at Fu'an.

Erection process

The construction process of *Chuandou* structures, which might be similar to that used in Dafuzhen, was photographed in Fujian in 2004. Transverse frames were assembled on the ground, and then erected one by one into vertical position. They were tied together by ridge purlins and longitudinal tie-beams to form an integrated structural framework.

Bibliography

Fujian Weiwu

Liang Wenbin, *Youxi Tubao* (Youxi Earthen Architecture), Fuzhou: Haixia Press, 2012.
Li Jianjun, *Fujian Sanming Tubaoqun* (Tubao at Sanming in Fujian), Fuzhou: Haixia Press, 2010.
Huang Chongyue, *Kejia Weiwu* (Hakka's Weiwu), Guangzhou: Huanan University Press, 2006.

Fengshui

He Xiaoxi, *Fengshui Tanyuan* (The Source of Fengshui). Nanjing: Southeast University Press, 1990.
Wang Junrong, *Yangzhai Shishu* (Ten Books on Fengshui), 16th century, reprint Shanghai: Jinzhang Bookstore, 1919.

Fujian vernacular

Chen Zhihua and He Congrong, *Xihuapian minju yu An'zhenbao* (Xihuapian Vernacular and An'zhenbao), Beijing: Tsinghua University Press, 2007.
Dai Zhijian, *Mintai Minju Jianzhu de Yuanyuan yu Xingtai* (History and Type of Fujian-Taiwan Vernacular), Fuzhou: Fujian People's Publishing House, 2003.
Fujian Heritage Committee, *Fujian Tulou*, Beijing: Encyclopaedia Publishing House, 2007.
Gao Zhenming, *Fujian Minju* (Fujian Vernacular), Beijing: China Building Industry Press, 1987.
Li Qiuxiang, *Fujian Minju* (Fujian Vernacular), Beijing: Tsinghua University Press, 2010.
Zhang Yuyu, *Fujian Chuangtong Damu Jiangshi Jiyi Yanjiu* (Studies on the Craftsmanship of Traditional Chinese Carpentry in Fujian Region). Nanjing: Southeast University Press, 2010.
Zeng Yidan, Fuzhou Gucuo (Traditional Housing in Fuzhou). Fuzhou: Fujian People's Publishing House, 2002.
Zheng Linwei, *Fujian Chuantong Jianzhu Gongyi Qiangjiuxing Yanjiu* (Fujian Traditional Construction Techniques, Master thesis), Southeast University, 2005.

Gaochi

Chen Yaodong, *Lubanjig Jiangjiajing Yanjiu* (Study on Lubanjing), Beijing: China Building Industry Press, 2010.

Vernacular

Li Jinsheng (de all ed.), *Shanxi Gucunzhen Lishi Jianzhu Cehui Tuji* (Measured Drawing of Traditional Vernacular in Shanxi). Beijing: China Building Industry Press, 2011.
Liu Dunzhen, *Zhongguo Zhuzhai Gaishuo* (Chinese Dwellings). Beijing: China Building Industry Press, 1957.
Wan Younan, *Gannan Weiwu Yanjiu* (Weiwu in South Jiangxi), Heilongjiang People's Publishing House, 2006.

Archaeology

Archaeological Institute of China, *Report and Research: Neolithic Settlement at Yuchisi in Mongcheng*, 2 vols. Beijing: Science Press 2007.
Zhouyuan Archaeological Team, »Brief Report of Excavation on a Palace Remains of the late Western Zhou at Fengchu, Shaanxi Province«, in: *Wenwu*, 1979, 10: 27–37.